Modes of Thought

Alfred North Whitehead

Modes
of
Thought

The Free Press, New York

Preface

The doctrine dominating these lectures is that factors in our experience are "clear and distinct" in proportion to their variability, provided that they sustain themselves for that moderate period required for importance. The necessities are invariable, and for that reason remain in the background of thought, dimly and vaguely. Thus philosophic truth is to be sought in the presuppositions of language rather than in its express statements. For this reason philosophy is akin to poetry, and both of them seek to express that ultimate good sense which we term civilization.

The first six chapters, namely Parts I and II, were delivered as lectures at Wellesley College, Masssachusetts, during the session 1937–38, succeeding my retirement from Harvard. This fortunate opportunity has helped me to condense for publication those features of my Harvard lectures which are incompletely presented in my published works. The two lectures of Part III, entitled "Nature and Life," were delivered four years earlier at the University of Chicago, and have been published by the University of Chicago Press, and in England by the Cambridge Press. They were meant to form part of a book such as the present one, but various circumstances have delayed the completion of the plan.

The Epilogue, "The Aim of Philosophy," is adapted from a short address at an annual reception, 1935, for graduate students of the Harvard and Radcliffe Philosophical Departments. It was reported in the Harvard Alumni Bulletin.

ALFRED NORTH WHITEHEAD

April 25, 1938

Contents

III.
NATURE AND LIFE

IV.
EPILOGUE

I.
CREATIVE IMPULSE

Importance

The first chapter in philosophic approach should consist in a free examination of some ultimate notions, as they occur naturally in daily life. I am referring to the generalities which are inherent in literature, in social organization, in the effort towards understanding physical occurrences.

There are no definitions of such notions. They are incapable of analysis in terms of factors more far-reaching than themselves. Each must be displayed as necessary to the various meanings of groups of notions, of equal depth with itself. In discussion of such a group any one of its members might, with slight adjustment of language, have been chosen as the central figure. In this lecture the notion of "Importance" has been taken as central, so that the discussion of a variety of topics comes back, time and again, to this idea.

In this whole set of lectures my aim is to examine some of those general characterizations of our experience which are presupposed in the directed activities of mankind. There will be no attempt to frame a systematic philosophy. Such a goal is too ambitious for a short course. All systematic thought must start from presuppositions. Also, as mentioned above—the discussion will incidentally employ more basic notions than are expressed in its explicit aim. The verbal expositions of such data must be trimmed, and dressed, and put in order, during any process of systematization.

In all systematic thought, there is a tinge of pedantry. There is a putting aside of notions, of experiences, and of suggestions, with the prim excuse that of course we are not thinking of such things. System is important. It is necessary for the handling, for the utilization, and for the criticism of the thoughts which throng into our experience.

But before the work of systematization commences, there is a previous task—a very necessary task if we are to avoid the narrownesses inherent in all finite systems. Today, even Logic itself is struggling with the discovery embodied in a formal proof, that every finite set of premises must indicate notions which are excluded from its direct purview. Philosophy can exclude nothing. Thus it should never start from systematization. Its primary stage can be termed *assemblage*.

Such a process is, of course, unending. All that can be achieved is the emphasis on a few large-scale notions, together with attention to the variety of other ideas which arise in the display of those chosen for primary emphasis. Systematic philosophy is a subject of study for specialists. On the other hand, the philosophic process of assemblage should have received some attention from every educated mind, in its escape from its own specialism.

In Western literature there are four great thinkers, whose services to civilized thought rest largely upon their achievements in philosophical assemblage; though each of them made important contributions to the structure of philosophic system. These men are Plato, Aristotle, Leibniz, and William James.

Plato grasped the importance of mathematical system;

but his chief fame rests upon the wealth of profound suggestions scattered throughout his dialogues, suggestions half smothered by the archaic misconceptions of the age in which he lived. Aristotle systematized as he assembled. He inherited from Plato, imposing his own systematic structures.

Leibniz inherited two thousand years of thought. He really did inherit more of the varied thoughts of his predecessors than any man before or since. His interests ranged from mathematics to divinity, and from divinity to political philosophy, and from political philosophy to physical science. These interests were backed by profound learning. There is a book to be written, and its title should be, *The Mind of Leibniz*.

Finally, there is William James, essentially a modern man. His mind was adequately based upon the learning of the past. But the essence of his greatness was his marvellous sensitivity to the ideas of the present. He knew the world in which he lived, by travel, by personal relations with its leading men, by the variety of his own studies. He systematized; but above all he assembled. His intellectual life was one protest against the dismissal of experience in the interest of system. He had discovered intuitively the great truth with which modern logic is now wrestling.

This prefatory discussion has been concerned with the two aspects of philosophy. Systematization is the criticism of generality by methods derived from the specialism of science. It presupposes a closed group of primary ideas. In another aspect philosophy is the entertainment of notions of large, adequate generality. Such a habit of mind is the very essence of civilization. It is civilization. The hermit thrush and the nightingale can produce sound of the utmost beauty. But they are not civilized beings. They lack ideas of adequate generality respecting their own actions and the world around them. Without doubt the higher animals entertain notions, hopes, and fears. And yet they lack civilization by reason of the deficient generality of their mental functionings. Their love, their devotion, their beauty of performance, rightly claim our love and our tenderness in return. Civilization is more than all these; and in moral worth it can be less than all these. Civilized beings are those who survey the world with some large generality of understanding.

2. There are two contrasted ideas which seem inevitably to underlie all width of experience, one of them is the notion of importance, the sense of importance, the presupposition of importance. The other is the notion of matter-of-fact. There is no escape from sheer matter-of-fact. It is the basis of importance; and importance is important because of the inescapable character of matter-of-fact. We concentrate by reason of a sense of importance. And when we concentrate, we attend to matter-of-fact. Those people who in a hard-headed way confine their attention to matter-of-fact do so by reason of their sense of the importance of such an attitude. The two notions are antithetical, and require each other.

One characteristic of the primary mode of conscious experience is its fusion of a large generality with an insistent particularity. There is a lack of precise analysis in the characterization of the particularities of experience. It is not true that the characterization of individual experience by qualitative notions commences with any detailed analysis of such quality. The basis of our primary consciousness of quality is a large generality. For example, characteristic modes of thought, as we first recall ourselves to civilized experience, are—"This is important," "That is difficult," "This is lovely."

In such ways of thinking there is an insistent particularity, symbolized above by the words *this* and *that;* and there is a large, vague characterization indicative of some

4

form of excitement arising from the particular fact in the world without. This vagueness is the despair of cultivated people. For the generality, when stated, is too obvious to be worth mentioning. And yet it is always there, just on the edge of consciousness. But good literature avoids the large philosophic generality which the quality exhibits. It fastens upon the accidental precision which inevitably clothes the qualitative generality. Literature is a curious mixture of tacitly presupposing analysis, and conversely of returning to emphasize explicitly the fundamental emotional importance of our naïve general intuitions.

Language is always relapsing into the generality of this intermediate stage between animal habit and learned precision. It is always degenerating into philosophic generality, under the guise of words capable of more precise use. Such a lapse is uneducated, because it expresses the obvious. And yet, it is philosophic; because the obvious embodies the permanent importance of variable detail. Literary people object to the vague use of words which are capable of precision.

For example, Coleridge, in his *Biographia Literaria,* objects to a party of tourists who gazed at a torrent and ejaculated "How pretty!" as a vague characterization of an awe-inspiring spectacle. Undoubtedly, in this instance, the degenerate phrase "How pretty!" lets down the whole vividness of the scene. And yet there is a real difficulty in the way of verbal expression. Words, in general, indicate useful particularities. How can they be employed to evoke a sense of that general character on which all importance depends? It is one function of great literature to evoke a vivid feeling of what lies beyond words.

3. Unfortunately for philosophy, learning tends to detail. Although in attempting to grasp our fundamental presuppositions, such as the contrast between "Importance" and "Matter-of-fact," we must undoubtedly have recourse

to the learning which we inherit; yet in the development of intelligence there is a great principle which is often forgotten. In order to acquire learning, we must first shake ourselves free of it. We must grasp the topic in the rough, before we smooth it out and shape it. For example, the mentality of John Stuart Mill was limited by his peculiar education which gave him system before any enjoyment of the relevant experience. Thus his systems were closed. We must be systematic; but we should keep our systems open. In other words, we should be sensitive to their limitations. There is always a vague beyond, waiting for penetration in respect to its detail.

The general notions which underlie the detailed thoughts of the modern Western civilizations of Europe and America are largely derived from the expressions of fundamental ideas bequeathed to us by the ancient world of Greeks, Semites, and Egyptians. All three sources emphasize the matter-of-fact world around us. But their emphasis of importance, as we have inherited from them, differs. From the Greeks our inheritance has been primarily aesthetic and logical; from the Semites it has been moral and religious; from the Egyptians it has been practical. The Greeks bequeathed enjoyment, the Semites worship, the Egyptians practical observation.

But this inheritance from the civilizations of the eastern Mediterranean has its special forms. Our notion of importance as a general factor in the universe has been restricted to these forms. It is the first task of modern philosophy to conceive of importance and matter-of-fact in some disengagement from the mentalities of the ancient world.

Matter-of-fact is the notion of mere existence. But when we seek to grasp this notion, it distinguishes itself into the subordinate notions of various types of existence— for example, fanciful or actual existences, and many other types. Thus the notion of existence involves the notion of an environment of existences and of types of existences. Any one instance of existence involves the notion of other existences, connected with it and yet beyond it. This notion of the environment introduces the notion of "more and less," and of multiplicity.

The notion of importance also refers to grades of importance and types of importance. Here again we reach the notion of more and less. Also something has to be important. There is no importance in a vacuum. Thus importance leads us back to matter-of-fact. But the multiplicity of matter-of-fact requires for a finite intellect selection in dealing with it. Now "selection" requires the notion of "this rather than that." Thus intellectual freedom issues from selection, and selection requires the notion of relative importance in order to give it meaning. Thus importance, selection, and intellectual freedom are bound up together, and they all involve some reference to matter-of-fact.

We have now been brought back to matter-of-fact. Let us again consider it for a while. The environment surpasses us in every physical dimension. Thus matter-of-fact is tinged with the notion of a compulsive determinism. The earth rotates; and we move with it, experiencing the routine of day and night as a prime necessity in our lives. The first Roman to mention the report of the midnight sun disbelieved it. He was an educated man well aware of the necessities of nature. In this way, the necessities of nature can be exaggerated. But all the same, in some sense or other they are there. In the same way, the freedom presupposed in the notion of selection is there, in some sense or other. Here we find an example of the value of a systematic philosophy. For we have either to explain the diverse senses in which freedom and necessity can coexist, or we have to explain away one or other of the most obvious presuppositions of our daily thoughts.

4. Let us set these two topics of matter-of-fact and of importance in another light.

The notion of mere matter-of-fact is the emergence into thought of the habit of mere existence to coördinate itself with the necessities of external activity. It is the recognition of the goings-on of nature in which we, and all things of all types, are immersed. It has its origin in the thought of ourselves as process immersed in process beyond ourselves. This grasp of factuality is one extreme of thought. Namely, it is the concept of mere agitation of things agitated.

This is the ideal of physical science, and it is the hidden ideal of those who insist upon the exclusive importance of objectivity.

The notion of importance is equally dominant in civilized thought. It can be inadequately defined as "Interest. involving that intensity of individual feeling which leads to publicity of expression." We are here trenching upon the topic of the next lecture. The definition is inadequate because there are two aspects to importance; one based on the unity of the Universe, the other on the individuality of the details. The word *interest* suggests the latter aspect; the word *importance* leans towards the former. In some sense or other interest always modifies expression. Thus, for the sake of reminding ourselves of this aspect of importance, the word *interest* will occasionally be used as a synonym. But importance is a fundamental notion not to be fully explained by any reference to a finite number of other factors.

As an explicit thought it is somewhat at odds with the concept of "Fact." A sound technological procedure is to analyse the facts in disregard of any subjective judgment as to their relative interest. And yet the notion of importance is like nature itself: Expel it with a pitchfork, and it ever returns. The most ardent upholders of objectivity in scientific thought insist upon its importance. In truth, "to uphold a doctrine" is itself such an insistence. Apart from a feeling of interest, you would merely notice the doctrine and not uphold it. The zeal for truth presupposes interest. Also sustained observation presupposes the notion. For concentrated attention means disregard of irrelevancies; and such disregard can only be sustained by some sense of importance.

Thus the sense of importance (or interest) is embedded in the very being of animal experience. As it sinks in dominance, experience trivializes and verges towards nothingness.

5. The notion of a mere fact is the triumph of the abstractive intellect. It has entered into the explicit thought of no baby and of no animal. Babies and animals are concerned with their wants as projected against the general environment. That is to say, they are immersed in their interest respecting details embedded in externality. There is the merest trace of the abstraction of the detail. A single fact in isolation is the primary myth required for finite thought, that is to say, for thought unable to embrace totality.

This mythological character arises because there is no such fact. Connectedness is of the essence of all things of all types. It is of the essence of types, that they be connected. Abstraction from connectedness involves the omission of an essential factor in the fact considered. No fact is merely itself. The penetration of literature and art at their height arises from our dumb sense that we have passed beyond mythology; namely, beyond the myth of isolation.

It follows that in every consideration of a single fact there is the suppressed presupposition of the environmental coördination requisite for its existence. This environment, thus coördinated, is the whole universe in its perspective to the fact. But perspective is gradation of relevance; that is to say, it is gradation of importance. Feeling is the agent which reduces the universe to its perspective for fact. Apart from gradations of feeling, the infinitude of detail produces an infinitude of effect in the constitution of each fact. And that is all that is to be said, when we omit feeling. But we feel differently about these effects and thus reduce them to a perspective. "To be negligible" means "to be negligible for some coördination of feeling." Thus perspective is the outcome of feeling; and feeling is graded by the sense of interest as to the variety of its differentiations.

In this way the finite intellect deals with the myth of finite facts. There can be no objection to this procedure, provided that we remember what we are doing. We are presupposing an environment which, in its totality, we are unable to define. For example, science is always wrong, so far as it neglects this limitation. The conjunction of premises, from which logic proceeds, presupposes that no difficulty will arise from the conjunction of the various unexpressed presuppositions involved in these premises. Both in science and in logic you have only to develop your argument sufficiently, and sooner or later you are bound to arrive at a contradiction, either internally within the argument, or externally in its reference to fact.

Judging from the history of European science, about three or four thousand years of continuous thought by a sufficient number of able people suffice to uncover some contradiction latent in any logical train of thought. As to physical science, the unguarded Newtonian doctrines survived for three hundred years. The span of life for modern scientific schemes is about thirty years. The father of European philosophy, in one of his many moods of thought, laid down the axiom that the deeper truths must be adumbrated by myths. Surely, the subsequent history of Western thought has amply justified his fleeting intuition.

It is to be noticed that none of these logical or scientific myths is wrong, in an unqualified sense of that term. It is unguarded. Its truth is limited by unexpressed presuppositions; and as time goes on we discover some of these limitations. The simpleminded use of the notions "right" or "wrong" is one of the chief obstacles to the progress of understanding.

6. Thus one characterization of importance is that it is that aspect of feeling whereby a perspective is imposed upon the universe of things felt. In our more self-conscious entertainment of the notion, we are aware of grading the effectiveness of things about us in proportion to their interest. In this way, we put aside, and we direct attention, and we perform necessary functions without bestowing the emphasis of conscious attention. The two notions of importance and of perspective are closely intertwined.

We may well ask whether the doctrine of perspective is not an endeavour to reduce the concept of importance to mere matter-of-fact devoid of intrinsic interest. Of course such reduction is impossible. But it is true to say that perspective is the dead abstraction of mere fact from the living importance of things felt. The concrete truth is the variation of interest; the abstraction is the universe in perspective; the consequent science is the scheme of physical laws which, with unexpressed presuppositions, expresses the patterns of perspective as observed by average human beings.

Importance is a generic notion which has been obscured by the overwhelming prominence of a few of its innumerable species. The terms *morality, logic, religion, art,* have each of them been claimed as exhausting the whole meaning of importance. Each of them denotes a subordinate species. But the genus stretches beyond any finite group of species. There are perspectives of the universe to which morality is irrelevant, to which logic is irrelevant, to which religion is irrelevant, to which art is irrelevant. By this false limitation the activity expressing the ultimate aim infused into the process of nature has been trivialized into the guardianship of mores, or of rules of thought, or of mystic sentiment, or of aesthetic enjoyment. No one of these specializations exhausts the final unity of purpose in the world. The generic aim of process is the attainment of importance, in that species and to that extent which in that instance is possible.

Of course the word *importance,* as in common use, has been reduced to suggest a silly little pomposity which is the extreme of trivialization of its meaning here. This is a permanent difficulty of philosophic discussion; namely, that words must be stretched beyond their common meanings in the marketplace. But notwithstanding this difficulty, philosophy must found itself upon the presuppositions and the interpretations of ordinary life. In our first approach to philosophy, learning should be banished. We should appeal to the simple-minded notions issuing from ordinary civilized social relations.

I will illustrate this doctrine by an anecdote of an incident which illustrated to me the possible irrelevance of moral considerations. About eleven years ago, a young friend of mine reached her tenth birthday. I will not guarantee the precise accuracy of these figures. Anyhow the young woman is now twenty-one and our friendship is still flourishing. The child's great-aunt celebrated the day by taking her to an afternoon performance of the opera Carmen, rendered in English. Also, she was allowed to select two companions for the treat. She chose another little girl and—I am proud to say—myself. As we came out of the opera house after the performance, she looked up at her aunt and said—"Auntie, do you think that those were *really good* people?" Both the aunt and I sidestepped the question by looking for the car which was to take us home.

The point that I now wish to make is that our enjoyment in the theatre was irrelevant to moral considerations applied to the performance. Of course smugglers are naughty people, and Carmen is carefree as to niceties of behaviour. But while they are singing their parts and dancing on the stage, morals vanish and beauty remains.

I am not saying that moral considerations are always irrelevant to the stage. In fact, sometimes they are the very topic of the play, especially of modern plays. But the retreat of morals in the presence of music, and of dancing, and the general gaiety of the theatre, is a fact very interesting to philosophers and very puzzling to the official censors.

7. The point is that moral codes are relevant to presuppositions respecting the systematic character of the relevant universe. When the presuppositions do not apply, that special code is a vacuous statement of abstract irrelevancies. We evade this difficulty as to codes by retaining their language with alterations of meaning introduced by the social changes within centuries and millennia. Also the inevitable imperfections of translation help in effecting the evasion. The translation has always to make sense in the epoch of the translators. The notion of the unqualified stability of particular laws of nature and of particular moral codes is a primary illusion which has vitiated much philosophy.

For example, consider the application of our moral notions concerning family relations to beings such as fish, who produce hundreds, nay thousands, of eggs in one year.

This conclusion as to moral codes must not be extended to involve the negation of any meaning to the term *morality*. In the same way, the notion of legality of behaviour within a state evades the possibility of complete codification. The legal profession can never be superseded by automata.

Morality consists in the control of process so as to

maximize importance. It is the aim at greatness of experience in the various dimensions belonging to it. This notion of the dimensions of experience, and of its importance in each dimension and of its final unity of importance, is difficult and hard to understand.

But only so far as we can adumbrate it, do we grasp the notion of morality. Morality is always the aim at that union of harmony, intensity, and vividness which involves the perfection of importance for that occasion. The codifications carry us beyond our own direct immediate insights. They involve the usual judgments valid for the usual occasions in that epoch. They are useful, and indeed essential, for civilization. But we only weaken their influence by exaggerating their status.

For example, consider the Ten Commandments. Can we really hold that a rest day once in seven days, as distinct from once in six or eight days, is an ultimate moral law of the universe? Can we really think that no work whatever can be done on Sundays? Can we really think that the division of time into days is an absolute factor in the nature of all existence? Evidently, the commandments are to be construed with common sense. In other words, they are formulations of behaviours which in ordinary circumstances, apart from very special reasons, it is better to adopt.

There is no one behaviour system belonging to the essential character of the universe, as the universal moral ideal. What is universal is the spirit which should permeate any behaviour system in the circumstances of its adoption. Thus morality does not indicate what you are to do in mythological abstractions. It does concern the general ideal which should be the justification for any particular objective. The destruction of a man, or of an insect, or of a tree, or of the Parthenon, may be moral or immoral. The Ten Commandments tell us that in the vast majority of cases such slaughter is better avoided. In these exceptional instances we avoid the term *murder*. Whether we destroy, or whether we preserve, our action is moral if we have thereby safeguarded the importance of experience so far as it depends on that concrete instance in the world's history.

8. Great advances in thought are often the result of fortunate errors. These errors are the result of oversimplification. The advance is due to the fact that, for the moment, the excess is not relevant to the use of the simplified notions. One of the chief examples of this truth is Aristotle's analysis into genus, and species, and sub-species. It was one of the happiest ideas possible, and it has clarified thinking ever since. Plato's doctrine of "division" was an anticipation, vague and hazy. He felt its value. It did not do much good, by reason of its lack of decisive clarity. Among sensible people, Aristotle's mode of analysis has been an essential feature in intellectual progress for two thousand years.

Of course, Plato was right and Aristotle was wrong. There is no clear division among genera; there is no clear division among species; there are no clear divisions anywhere. That is to say, there are no clear divisions when you push your observations beyond the presuppositions on which they rest. It so happens, however, that we always think within limitations.

As a practical question, Aristotle was right and Plato was muddled, But, what neither Aristotle nor Plato adequately conceived was the necessity for investigation of the peculiar characterization of that sense of importance which is current in the thought of each age. All classification depends on the current character of importance.

We have now behind us some detailed history of three or four thousand years of civilization. The Greeks (as Thucydides discloses) were ignorant of history, except for that of two or three almost contemporaneous generations.

The Egyptians and the Jews worshipped a long history, uncritically. The Greeks would have criticized history, if they had known anything about it; the Jews would have criticized history, if they had not worshipped its records; the Egyptians would have criticized history, if they had not been sensible men who confined themselves to "pure history." By the same exercise of good sense, the Egyptians failed to generalize their geometrical knowledge, and thus lost their chance to become the founders of modern civilization. An excess of common sense has its disadvantages. The Greeks, with their airy generalizations, were always children—very fortunately for the modern world. Panic of error is the death of progress; and love of truth is its safeguard.

9. For these reasons, the criticism of history has been left for development by the modern world of the last four centuries. Of course there is no sudden beginning. Anticipations of such criticism can always be found in the older literature. Yet it remains true that modern thought is remarkable for its concentration of attention upon history. This criticism has itself passed through phases.

The first emphasis was upon the authenticity of the record. Such questions as, Did Plato write this dialogue?, Did the Emperor Constantine make this donation?, were the primary topics. This phase of correction passed to details. It was then called "emendation." Is this manuscript of the *Aeneid* a correct version of what Virgil wrote? This is a fairly definite question. But the relation of Homer to the *Iliad* is vaguer. Perhaps Homer and his comrades could not write. Even if they could write, they were very unlikely to have written down the *Iliad*. Papyrus was scarce, and it was easier to remember it. Thus the poem was handed down through generations of groups of bards with a sublime indifference to minor variations. Later we have records of formal revisions of the text. Analogous vagueness applies to the concepts of all social transactions. Thus the notion of accurate record has its limitations.

History has now passed into another phase. It is displaying transitions of behaviour. The Western historian is depicting types of activity, types of mood, and types of formulated belief, exhibited in the adventures of the European races as they overran first Europe, then America, and the fringes of other continents and islands. This change in emphasis showed itself decidedly in the eighteenth century.

For example, Bentley, the typical scholarly critic, died in 1742; and Gibbon, who traced the decline and fall of a political system, and the variations of motive animating its activity, was born in 1737. Gibbon corrected no editions of authors, and Bentley depicted no transitions of behaviour. In Europe, the change may be symbolized by Mabillon, who died in 1707, and Voltaire, who was born in 1694. Of course historical phases overlap each other. I am speaking of predominant interest. In the earlier period, even the discursive humanist, Erasmus, issued accurate editions; in the nineteenth century historical narrative was more prominent than devotion to editorial accuracy. Of course there were reasons for the change, and all the types of historic scholarship co-exist.

Under the influence of physical science, the task of history has more recently been limited to the narration of mere sequences. This ideal of knowledge is the triumph of matter-of-fact. Such suggestion of causation, as is admitted, is confined to the statements of physical materialities, such as the economic motive.

Such history confines itself to abstract mythology. The variety of motives is excluded. You cannot write the history of religious development without estimate of the motive-power of religious belief. The history of the Papacy is not a mere sequence of behaviours. It illustrates a mode of causation, which is derived from a mode of thought.

Thus the study of history as mere sequence wears itself out. It is a make-belief. There are oceans of facts. We seek that thread of coordination derived from the special forms of importance prevalent in the respective epochs. Apart from such interests, intrinsic within each period, there would be no language, no art, no heroism, no devotion. Ideals lie beyond matter-of-fact, and yet provide the colour of its development.

10. Matter-of-fact is an abstraction, arrived at by confining thought to purely formal relations which then masquerade as the final reality. This is why science, in its perfection, relapses into the study of differential equations. The concrete world has slipped through the meshes of the scientific net.

Consider, for example, the scientific notion of measurement. Can we elucidate the turmoil of Europe by weighing its dictators, its prime ministers, and its editors of newspapers? The idea is absurd, although some relevant information might be obtained. I am not upholding the irrelevance of science. Such a doctrine would be foolish. For example, a daily record of the bodily temperatures of the men, above mentioned, might be useful. My point is the incompleteness of the information.

Each social system is realizing a variety of modes of interest, some of them dominant, and some in the background. The eighteenth century was not merely the age of reason, nor was the sixteenth century merely the age of religious excitement. For example, to study the Reformation turmoil without reference to America, and to India, and to the Turks, and to the rise of nationalism, and to the recent diffusion of printing, is ridiculous. The relevance of these factors consists in their modifications of prevalent modes of importance, which interfused with the religious interest.

The chequered history of religion and morality is the main reason for the widespread desire to put them aside in favour of the more stable generalities of science. Unfortunately for this smug endeavour to view the universe as the incarnation of the commonplace, the impact of aesthetic, religious and moral notions is inescapable. They are the disrupting and the energizing forces of civilization. They force mankind upwards and downwards. When their vigour abates, a slow mild decay ensues. Then new ideals arise, bringing in their train a rise in the energy of social behaviour.

The concentration of attention upon matter-of-fact is the supremacy of the desert. Any approach to such triumph bestows on learning a fugitive, and a cloistered virtue, which shuns emphasis on essential connections such as disclose the universe in its impact upon individual experience.

Expression

This lecture is concerned with various ideas involved in the notion of "Expression." The more general notion of importance is presupposed by expression. Something is to be diffused throughout the environment which will make a difference. But there is a distinction between the two notions. Importance is primarily monistic in its reference to the universe. Importance, limited to a finite individual occasion, ceases to be important. In some sense or other, importance is derived from the immanence of infinitude in the finite.

But expression is founded on the finite occasion. It is the activity of finitude impressing itself on its environment. Thus it has its origin in the finite; and it represents the immanence of the finite in the multitude of its fellows beyond itself. The two together, namely importance and expression, are witnesses both to the monistic aspect of the universe and to its pluralistic character. Importance passes from the world as one to the world as many; whereas, expression is the gift from the world as many to the world as one.

Selection belongs to expression. A mood of the finite thing conditions the environment. There is an active entity which fashions its own perspective, implanted on the world around. The laws of nature are large average effects which reign impersonally. Whereas, there is nothing average about expression. It is essentially individual. In so far as an average dominates, expression fades.

Expression is the diffusion, in the environment, of something initially entertained in the experience of the expressor. No conscious determination is necessarily involved; only the impulse to diffuse. This urge is one of the simplest characteristics of animal nature. It is the most fundamental evidence of our presupposition of the world without.

In fact, the world beyond is so intimately entwined in our own natures that unconsciously we identify our more vivid perspectives of it with ourselves. For example, our bodies lie beyond our own individual existence. And yet they are part of it. We think of ourselves as so intimately entwined in bodily life that a man is a complex unity—body and mind. But the body is part of the external world, continuous with it. In fact, it is just as much part of nature as anything else there—a river, or a mountain, or a cloud. Also, if we are fussily exact, we cannot define where a body begins and where external nature ends.

Consider one definite molecule. It is part of nature. It has moved about for millions of years. Perhaps it started from a distant nebula. It enters the body; it may be as a factor in some edible vegetable; or it passes into the lungs as part of the air. At what exact point as it enters the mouth, or as it is absorbed through the skin, is it part of the body? At what exact moment, later on, does it cease to be part of the body? Exactness is out of the question. It can only be obtained by some trivial convention.

Thus we arrive at this definition of our bodies: The human body is that region of the world which is the primary field of human expression.

For example, anger issues into bodily excitements, which are then publicized in the form of appropriate language, or in other modes of violent action. We can leave it to the physiologists, in the various departments of that science, to analyse the special sorts of bodily functioning thus elicited. Philosophy should refrain from trespassing upon specialist investigations. Its business is to point out fields for research. Some fields remain untilled for centuries. The fruitful initiation is absent, or perhaps interest has never concentrated upon them.

In the present instance, we have defined an animal body—for the higher grade of animals—and have indicated the sort of researches required. Of course, mankind has been engaged on this job for some thousands of years, with some lack of comprehension of its full import. It is the business of philosophy to elicit this consciousness; and then, to coördinate the results of all such specialist enquiries.

So far, we have been considering the bodies of animals with dominant centres of feeling and of expression. We can now enlarge the definition so as to include all living bodies, animal and vegetable:—

Wherever there is a region of nature which is itself the primary field of the expressions issuing from each of its parts, that region is alive.

In this second definition, the phrase "expressions issuing from each of its parts" has been substituted for the phrase "human expression," as used previously. The new definition is wider than the former by extending beyond human beings, and beyond the higher animals. Also it will be noticed that these definitions involve the direct negation of any extreme form of Behaviourism. In such behaviouristic doctrines, importance and expression must be banished and can never be intelligently employed. A consistent behaviourist cannot feel it important to refute my statements. He can only behave.

There are two sides to an animal body of the higher type, and so far we have only developed one of them. The second, and wider, definition enables us to find the distinction between vegetation and animal life. This distinction, like others, refuses to be pushed to meticulous exactness. In the animal, there is the one experience expressing itself throughout the animal body. But this is only half the tale.

The other half of the tale is that the body is composed of various centres of experience imposing the expression of themselves on each other. Feeling (in the sense here used), or prehension, is the reception of expressions. Thus the animal body is composed of entities, which are mutually expressing and feeling. Expressions are the data for feeling diffused in the environment; and a living body is a peculiarly close adjustment of these two sides of experience, namely, expression and feeling. By reason of this organization, an adjusted variety of feelings is produced in that supreme entity which is the one animal considered as one experiencing subject.

Thus the one animal, and the various parts of its body considered as themselves centres of experience, are in one sense on a level. Namely, they are centres of experience expressing themselves vividly to each other, and obtaining their own feelings mainly by reason of such mutual expressions.

In another sense, the animal as one centre of experience is on a higher level than its other bodily centres. For these subordinate centres are specialists. They only receive restricted types of emotional feeling, and are impervious beyond such types. Throughout the body there is a complex coördination of a vast variety of emotional types. The bodily organization is such that the unity of feeling, which is the one animal as a sentient being, receives its complex variety of experience from these bodily activities. Thus the combined data for feeling in the animal centre are on a higher level than are the corresponding data for its other bodily centres.

In the case of vegetables, we find bodily organizations which decisively lack any one centre of experience with a higher complexity either of expressions received or of inborn data. A vegetable is a democracy; an animal is dominated by one, or more centres of experience. But such domination is limited, very strictly limited. The expressions of the central leader are relevant to that leader's reception of data from the body.

Thus an animal body exhibits the limited domination of at least one of its component activities of expression. If the dominant activity be severed from the rest of the body, the whole coördination collapses, and the animal dies. Whereas in the case of the vegetable, the democracy can be subdivided into minor democracies which easily survive without much apparent loss of functional expression.

It is evident that our statement is oversimplified. In the first place, the distinction between animals and vegetables is not sharp cut. Some traces of dominance can be observed in vegetables, and some traces of democratic independence can be found in animals. For example, portions of an animal body preserve their living activities when severed from the main body. But there is failure in variety of energy and in survival power. Yet allowing for such failure, the vegetable characteristics of equality and independence do manifest themselves. Thus ordinary vegetation and the higher animals represent extremes in the bewildering variety of bodily formations which we term *living things*.

Then we have neglected the differentiation of functions which are to be found alike in vegetables and animals. In the case of the flora, there are the roots, and the branches, and the leaves, and the flowers, and the seeds—all obvious to common inspection. And the detailed observations of botanists supplement these blatant examples of differentiation by a hundred other functional activities which constitute the physiology of plant life.

When we turn to the animal body, the notion of the sole domination of the directing experience requires limitation. There are subordinate agencies which have essential control of the bodily functioning. The heart is one example among many others. The activities of the heart are necessary to the bodily survival, in a way that contrasts with the feet. A foot can be severed with slight damage to the internal functioning; the heart is essential. Thus an animal body in its highest examples is more analogous to a feudal society, with its one overlord.

This final unity of animal intelligence is also the organ of reaction to novel situations, and is the organ introducing the requisite novelty of reaction. Finally, the overlord tends to relapse into the conventionality of routine imposed upon the subordinate governors, such as the heart. Animal life can face conventional novelties with conventional devices. But the governing principle lacks large power for the sudden introduction of any major novelty.

The bodies of the higher animals have some resemblance to a complex society of insects, such as ants. But the individual insects seem to have more power of adaptation to their problems than does the community as a whole. The opposite holds in the case of animals. For example, an intelligent dog has more power of adaptation to new modes of life than has its heart, as it functions in the animal body. The dog can be trained, but its heart must go its own way within very close limits.

When we come to mankind, nature seems to have burst through another of its boundaries. The central activity of enjoyment and expression has assumed a reversal in the importance of its diverse functionings. The conceptual entertainment of unrealized possibility becomes a major factor in human mentality. In this way outrageous novelty is introduced, sometimes beatified, sometimes damned, and sometimes literally patented or protected by copyright. The definition of mankind is that in this genus of animals the central activity has been developed on the side of its relationship to novelty. This relationship is two-fold. There is the novelty received from the aggregate diversities of bodily expressions. Such novelty requires decision as to its reduction to coherence of expression.

Again there is the introduction of novelty of feeling by the entertainment of unexpressed possibilities. This second side is the enlargement of the conceptual experience of mankind. The characterization of this conceptual feeling is the sense of what might be and of what might have been. It is the entertainment of the alternative. In its highest development, this becomes the entertainment of the ideal. It emphasizes the sense of importance, discussed in the previous lecture. And this sense exhibits itself in various species, such as, the sense of morality, the mystic sense of religion, the sense of that delicacy of adjustment which is beauty, the sense of necessity for mutual connection which is understanding, and the sense of discrimination of each factor which is consciousness.

Also it is the nature of feeling to pass into expression. Thus the expression of these various feelings produces the history of mankind as distinct from the narrative of animal behaviours. History is the record of the expressions of feelings peculiar to humanity.

There is, however, every gradation of transition between animals and men. In animals we can see emotional feeling, dominantly derived from bodily functions, and yet tinged with purposes, hopes, and expression derived from conceptual functioning. In mankind, the dominant dependence on bodily functioning seems still there. And yet the life of a human being receives its worth, its importance, from the way in which unrealized ideals shape its purposes and tinge its actions. The distinction between men and animals is in one sense only a difference in degree. But the extent of the degree makes all the difference. The Rubicon has been crossed.

Thus in nature we find four types of aggregations of actualities: the lowest is the nonliving aggregation, in which mutual influence is predominantly of a formal character expressible in formal sciences, such as mathematics. The inorganic is dominated by the average. It lacks individual expression in its parts. Their flashes of selection (if any) are sporadic and ineffective. Its parts merely transmit average expressions; and thus the structure survives. For the average is always there, stifling individuality.

The vegetable grade exhibits a democracy of purposeful influences issuing from its parts. The predominant aim within the organism is survival for its own coördinated individual expressiveness. This expressiveness has a large average character. But the nature of this average is dominated by the intricacies of its own bodily formation. It has added coördinated, organic individuality to the impersonal average formality of inorganic nature. What is merely latent potentiality in lifeless matter, has awakened into some realization in the vegetable. But in each instance of vegetation, the total bodily organism strictly limits the individuality of expression in the parts.

The animal grade includes at least one central actuality, supported by the intricacy of bodily functioning. Purposes transcending (however faintly) the mere aim at survival are exhibited. For animal life the concept of importance, in some of its many differentiations, has a real relevance. The human grade of animal life immensely extends this concept, and thereby introduces novelty of functioning as essential for varieties of importance. Thus morals and religion arise as aspects of this human impetus towards the best in each occasion. Morals can be discerned in the higher animals; but not religion. Morality emphasizes the detailed occasion; while religion emphasizes the unity of ideal inherent in the universe.

In every grade of social aggregation, from a nonliving material society up to a human body, there is the necessity for expression. It is by reason of average expression, and of average reception, that the average activities of merely material bodies are restrained into conformity with the reigning laws of nature. It is by reason of individual expression and reception that the human body exhibits activities expressive of the intimate feelings, emotional and purposeful, of the one human person.

3. These bodily activities are very various and intensely selective. An angry man, except when emotion has swamped other feelings, does not usually shake his fist at the universe in general. He makes a selection and knocks his neighbour down. Whereas a piece of rock impartially attracts the universe according to the law of gravitation.

The impartiality of physical science is the reason for its failure as the sole interpreter of animal behaviour. It is true that the rock falls on one special patch of earth. This happens, because the universe in that neighbourhood is exemplifying one particular solution of a differential equation. The fist of the man is directed by emotion seeking a novel feature in the universe, namely, the collapse of his opponent. In the case of the rock, the formalities predominate. In the case of the man, explanation must seek the individual satisfactions. These enjoyments are constrained by formalities, but in proportion to their intensities they pass beyond them, and introduce individual expression.

Consciousness is the first example of the selectiveness of enjoyment in the higher animals. It arises from expression coördinating the activities of physiological functionings. There is a baseless notion that we consciously observe those activities of nature which are dominant in our neighbourhood. The exact opposite is the case. The animal consciousness does not easily discriminate its dependence on detailed bodily functioning. Such discrimination is usually a sign of illness. When we observe the functionings of our viscera, something has gone wrong. We take the infinite complexity of our bodies for granted.

The first principle of epistemology should be that the changeable, shifting aspects of our relations to nature are the primary topics for conscious observation. This is only common sense; for something can be done about them. The organic permanences survive by their own momentum: our hearts beat, our lungs absorb air, our blood circulates, our stomachs digest. It requires advanced thought to fix attention on such fundamental operations.

The higher animals have developed superficial relationships to nature, such as eyesight, hearing, smell, and taste. Also such connections are alterable in proportion to their high-grade character. For example, we have only got to shut our eyes, and visual experience has vanished. We can block our ears, and there is no hearing.

The experiences on which accurate science bases itself

are completely superficial. The blind and the deaf are capable of the ultimate greatness of human life. They are deprived of its walking sticks. The traffic lights on the highways are useful for the accomplishment of modern purposes. And yet there have been great civilizations without motor cars, and without traffic lights.

But though any one of these sense experiences is nonessential to the existence of the organism, the whole group is quite essential for the development of the higher forms of animal life. Mankind and the animals with analogous abilities are distinguished by their capacity for the introduction of novelty. This requires a conceptual power which can imagine, and a practical power which can effect. The role of sense experiences consists in the fact that they are manageable.

The animals evolved and emphasized the superficial aspects of their connexity with nature, and thus obtained a manageable grip upon the world. The central organism which is the soul of a man is mainly concerned with the trivialities of human existence. It does not easily meditate upon the activities of fundamental bodily functions. Instead of fixing attention on the bodily digestion of vegetable food, it catches the gleam of the sunlight as it falls on the foliage. It nurtures poetry. Men are the children of the Universe, with foolish enterprises and irrational hopes. A tree sticks to its business of mere survival; and so does an oyster with some minor divergencies. In this way, the life aim at survival is modified into the human aim at survival for diversified worthwhile experience.

The pitfall of philosophy is exclusive concentration on these manageable relationships, to the neglect of the underlying necessities of nature. Thus thinkers repudiate our intimate vague experiences in favour of a mere play of distinct sensations, coupled with a fable about underlying reality. I am now pleading that our whole experience is composed out of our relationships to the rest of things, and of the formation of new relationships constitutive of things to come. The present receives the past and builds the future. But there are grades of permanence and of compulsive stability.

During many generations there has been an attempt to explain our ultimate insights as merely interpretive of sense impressions. Indeed this school of thought can trace itself back to Epicurus. It can appeal to some phrases of Plato. I suggest to you that this basis for philosophic understanding is analogous to an endeavour to elucidate the sociology of modern civilization as wholly derivative from the traffic signals on the main roads. The motions of the cars are conditioned by these signals. But the signals are not the reasons for the traffic. Common sense supplies this conclusion, so overwhelmingly that illustration is unnecessary.

It is this direct insight, vague as to detail and yet the basis of all rationality, that has been denied by the prevalent epistemology of the preceding century. Interest and importance are the primary reasons for the effort after exact discrimination of sense data. The traffic signals are the outcome of the traffic.

Importance generates interest. Interest leads to discrimination. In this way, interest is increased; and the two factors, interest and discrimination, stimulate each other. Finally consciousness develops, gradually and fitfully; and it becomes another agent of stimulation.

4. In this lecture, the dominant topic is expression. Accordingly, we now pass to the outstanding example of the way in which mankind has fabricated its manageable connections with the world into a means of expression. Language is the triumph of human ingenuity, surpassing even

the intricacies of modern technology. It tells of widespread intelligence, sustained throughout scores of thousands of years. It is interesting that from the alternatives, sight and sound, sound was the medium first developed. There might have been a language of gesticulation. Indeed, there is a trace of it. But the weak point of gesticulation is that one cannot do much else while indulging in it. The advantage of sound is that the limbs are left free while we produce it.

But there is a deeper reason for the unconscious recourse to sound production. Hands and arms constitute the more unnecessary parts of the body. We can do without them. They do not excite the intimacies of bodily existence. Whereas in the production of sound, the lungs and throat are brought into play. So that in speech, while a superficial, manageable expression is diffused, yet the sense of the vague intimacies of organic existence is also excited. Thus voice-produced sound is a natural symbol for the deep experiences of organic existence.

This sense of reality is of great importance for the effectiveness of symbolism. Personal interviews carry more weight than gramophone records. What an economy could be achieved if the faculties of colleges could be replaced by fifty gramophones and a few thousand records! Indeed, we might have expected that in the sixteenth century printed books would have replaced universities. On the contrary, the sixteenth and seventeenth centuries were an active period in the development of educational foundations. The sense of reality can never be adequately sustained amidst mere sensa, either of sound or sight. The connexity of existence is of the essence of understanding.

Language has two functions. It is converse with another, and it is converse with oneself. The latter function is too often overlooked, so we will consider it first. Language is expression from one's past into one's present. It is the reproduction in the present of sensa which have intimate association with the realities of the past. Thus the experience of the past is rendered distinct in the present, with a distinctness borrowed from the well-defined sensa. In this way, an articulated memory is the gift of language, considered as an expression from oneself in the past to oneself in the present.

Again by the aid of a common language, the fragmentary past experiences of the auditor, as enshrined in words, can be recombined into a novel imaginative experience by the reception of the coherent sentences of the speaker. Thus in both functions of language the immediate imaginative experience is enormously increased, and is stamped with a sense of realization, or of possible realization.

When we examine the content of language, that is to say, the experiences which it symbolizes, it is remarkable how largely it points away from the abstractions of high-grade sensa. Its meaning presupposes the concrete relations of real events happening and issuing from each other. What Descartes, in his *Meditations*, terms a "Realitas Objectiva" clings to most sentences, especially to those recording the simpler experiences.

Consider, for example, the homely illustration, used earlier in this lecture, of the angry man who knocks his neighbour down. We each of us frame a pictorial imagination of such a scene. But the flux of imagined sensa is not of the essence of our thought. The event may have generated sensory schemes in a thousand ways. It may have happened by day, or by night. It may have happened in the street, or in a room. Every variety of attitudes for victor and for vanquished is indifferent. Yet amid all this ambiguity of sensa, the stubborn flux of events is asserted, that the fist of the angry man completely upset the stable functioning of his victim's body. It is not a flux of sensa which is asserted, but a bodily collapse as the result of the expressiveness of the angry man.

Also the anger of the man undoubtedly affected the functioning of his own body. A careful physiological examination with a microscope could have yielded many visual sensa to an observer! Again, consider the variety of sensory pictures which are aroused by the notion of one man knocking another down. What is it that binds them together? In themselves, they are merely different compositions of visual sensa. Their unity consists in the type of connected process in the world that they suggest.

Deserting this special example, different sensory experiences derived from the same action have a unity, namely, in the identity of the action. The accounts may be in different languages and may fasten upon different transitions of visual or auditory sensa; and yet they refer to the same action. Also the action may not be purely physical. Heroism, and courage, and love, and hatred are possible characteristics of things that happen.

The essence of language is that it utilizes those elements in experience most easily abstracted for conscious entertainment, and most easily reproduced in experience. By the long usage of humanity, these elements are associated with their meanings which embrace a large variety of human experiences. Each language embalms an historic tradition. Each language is the civilization of expression in the social systems which use it. Language is the systematization of expression.

Of all the ways of expressing thought, beyond question language is the most important. It has been held even that language is thought, and that thought is language. Thus a sentence is the thought. There are many learned works in which this doctrine is tacitly presupposed; and in not a few it is explicitly stated.

If this extreme doctrine of language be adopted, it is difficult to understand how translation from language to language, or within the same language between alternative sentences, is possible. If the sentence is the thought, then another sentence is another thought. It is true that no translation is perfect. But how can the success of imperfection be achieved when not a word, or a syllable, or an order of succession is the same? If you appeal to grammar, you are appealing to a meaning which lies behind words, syllables, and orders of succession. Some of us struggle to find words to express our ideas. If the words and their order together constitute the ideas, how does the struggle arise? We should then be struggling to obtain ideas; whereas we are conscious of ideas verbally unexpressed.

Let it be admitted then that language is not the essence of thought. But this conclusion must be carefully limited. Apart from language, the retention of thought, the easy recall of thought, the interweaving of thought into higher complexity, the communication of thought, are all gravely limited. Human civilization is an outgrowth of language, and language is the product of advancing civilization. Freedom of thought is made possible by language: we are thereby released from complete bondage to the immediacies of mood and circumstance. It is no accident that the Athenians from whom we derive our Western notions of freedom enjoyed the use of a language supreme for its delicate variety.

The denial that language is of the essence of thought, is not the assertion that thought is possible apart from the other activities coördinated with it. Such activities may be termed the expression of thought. When these activities satisfy certain conditions, they are termed a language. The whole topic of these lectures is the discussion of the interdependence of thought and its expressive activities.

Such activities, emotional and physical, are older than thought. They existed in our ancestors when thought slumbered in embryo. Thought is the outcome of its own concurrent activities; and having thus arrived upon the scene, it modifies and adapts them. The notion of pure thought in abstraction from all expression is a figment of the learned world. A thought is a tremendous mode of excitement. Like a stone thrown into a pond it disturbs the whole surface of our being. But this image is inadequate. For we should conceive the ripples as effective in the creation of the plunge of the stone into the water. The ripples release the thought, and the thought augments and distorts the ripples. In order to understand the essence of thought we must study its relation to the ripples amid which it emerges.

5. Nevertheless, putting aside these refinements as to the origins and effects of thought, language, as commonly understood in the most simple-minded way, stands out as the habitual effect of thought, and the habitual revelation of thought. In order to understand the modes of thought we must endeavour to recall the psychology which has produced the civilization of language—or, if you prefer to invert the expression, the language of civilization.

The first point to notice is that we now employ two distinct types of language, namely, the language of sound and the language of sight. There is speech, and there is writing. The language of writing is very modern. Its history extends for less than ten thousand years, even if we allow for the faint anticipations of writing in the primitive pictures. But writing as an effective instrument of thought, with widespread influence, may be given about five or six thousand years at the most.

Writing as a factor in human experience is comparable to the steam engine. It is important, modern, and artificial. Speech is as old as human nature itself. It is one of the primary factors constituting human nature. We must not exaggerate. It is now possible to elicit the full stretch of human experience by other devices when speech in exceptional instances is denied. But speech, developing as a general social acquirement, was one leading creative factor in the uprise of humanity. Speech is human nature itself, with none of the artificiality of written language.

Finally, we now so habitually intermingle writing and speech in our daily experience that, when we discuss language, we hardly know whether we refer to speech, or to writing, or to the mixture of both. But this final mixture is very modern. About five hundred years ago, only a small minority could read—at least among the European races. That is one great reason for the symbolism of religion, and for the pictorial signs of inns and of shops. The armorial bearings of great nobles were a substitute for writing. The effect of writing on the psychology of language is a neglected chapter in the history of civilization.

Speech, in its embryonic stage as exemplified in animal and human behaviour, varies between emotional expression and signalling. In the course of such variation it rapidly becomes a mixture of both. Throughout its most elaborate developments, speech retains these three characterizations, namely, emotional expression, signalling, and interfusion of the two. And yet somehow in the intellectualized language of advanced civilizations, these characteristics seem to fade into the background. They suggest something which has lost its dominating position. We cannot understand modes of thought in the recent civilizations of the last thirty centuries unless we attend to this subtle change in the function of language. The presuppositions of language are various.

Language arose with a dominating reference to an immediate situation. Whether it was signal or expression, above all things it was *this* reaction to *that* situation in *this* environment. In the origin of language the particularity of the immediate present was an outstanding element in the meaning conveyed. The genus *bird* remained in the background of undiscerned meaning; even these particular birds on some other occasion were but dimly sensed. What language primarily conveyed was the direction of attention to these birds, here, now, amid these surroundings.

Language has gradually achieved the abstraction of its meanings from the presupposition of any particular environment. The fact that the French dictionary is published in Paris, at a definite date, is irrelevant to the meanings of the words as explained in the dictionary. The French equivalent to the English word *green,* means just green, whatever be the state of Europe, or of the planetary system. Green is green, and there is the end of it. There is nothing more to be said, when you once understand the word in reference to its meaning.

Of course, we are much more civilized than our ancestors who could merely think of green in reference to some particular spring morning. There can be no doubt about our increased powers of thought, of analysis, of recollection, and of conjecture. We cannot congratulate ourselves too warmly on the fact that we are born among people who can talk about green in abstraction from springtime. But at this point we must remember the warning—Nothing too much.

So long as language is predominantly speech, the reference to some particularity of environment is overwhelming. Consider the simple phrase "a warm day." In a book, as interpreted by a standard dictionary, the words have a generalised meaning which refers to the rotation of the earth, the existence of the sun, and the scientific doctrine of temperature. Now put aside the dictionary, and forget all scraps of science. Then, with this abstraction from learning, the experience indicated by the ejaculation "a warm day" is very different for speakers in Texas, or on the coast of England bordering the North Sea. And yet there is an identity of meaning. Nothing too much.

We have to understand language as conveying the identities on which knowledge is based, and as presupposing the particularity of reference to the environment which is the essence of existence. Spoken language is immersed in the immediacy of social intercourse. Written language lies hidden in a volume, to be opened and read at diverse times and in diverse places, in abstraction from insistent surroundings. But a book can be read aloud. Here we find an instance of the fusion of writing and speech. Reading aloud is an art, and the reader makes a great difference. The immediacy of the environment then enters into the abstraction of writing.

The abstraction, inherent in the development of language, has its dangers. It leads away from the realities of the immediate world. Apart from a balanced emphasis, it ends in the triviality of quick-witted people. And yet, for all its dangers, this abstraction is responsible for the final uprise of civilization. It gives expression to the conceptual experiences, latent throughout nature, although kept under by vast conformity to average matter-of-fact. In mankind, these conceptual experiences are coördinated, and express themselves throughout their environment. This coördination has two aspects, aesthetic and logical. These aspects will form the topic of my next lecture.

In conclusion, it is time to sum up what I have been saying this afternoon. This lecture is nothing else than a modern rendering of the oldest of civilized reflections on the development of the universe as seen from the perspective of life on this earth. In comparing modern thought with ancient records, we must remember the difficulties of translation, and the difficulties of any thinker battling with the verbal expression of thought which penetrates below the ordinary usages of the market place. For instance, how differently would Aristotle's metaphysical reflections read if we persisted in translating one of his metaphysical key words by the English term *wood,* and also insisted on giving the most literal meaning to that word. There is evidence that three thousand years ago there were deep thinkers, enmeshed as to their imaginations in the trivial modes of presentation belonging to their own days.

But we can discern in the records, which have been edited and re-edited by unimaginative scribes, the notion of the evolution of the universe as viewed from the perspective of life on this earth. We can discern the classification, involving the large physical grades, the grades of vegetation and of animal life, the final rise to human life.

We can also discern the notion of the interweaving of language with the rise of human experience, in the naïve, childish account of the naming of things. In fact, the whole ancient account is simple-minded in the extreme. And yet the pretentious generalities of the modern rendering do not attain much more than an endeavour to avoid the over-sharp divisions between the various stages, and the excessive simplification of.the agencies involved.

This lecture has been written in terms of immanence, and in terms of action and reaction. Its final conclusion respecting human nature, is that the mentality of mankind and the language of mankind created each other. If we like to assume the rise of language as a given fact, then it is not going too far to say that the souls of men are the gift from language to mankind.

The account of the sixth day should be written, He gave them speech, and they became souls.

Understanding

In the two foregoing lectures, importance and expression have been discussed. The notion of "Understanding" is the third of the trilogy, upon which we base our endeavour to analyze the intelligence of mankind. Our quest is to understand understanding.

I submit to you that in its full extent this is a hopeless task. We can enlighten fragmentary aspects of intelligence. But there is always an understanding beyond our area of comprehension. The reason is that the notion of intelligence in pure abstraction from things understood is a myth. Thus a complete understanding is a perfect grasp of the universe in its totality. We are finite beings; and such a grasp is denied to us.

This is not to say that there are finite aspects of things which are intrinsically incapable of entering into human knowledge. Whatever exists, is capable of knowledge in respect to the finitude of its connections with the rest of things. In other words, we can know anything in some of its perspectives. But the totality of perspectives involves an infinitude beyond finite knowledge. For example, we know about the colour *green* in some of its perspectives. But what green is capable of in other epochs of the universe, when other laws of nature are reigning, is beyond our present imaginations. And yet there is nothing intrinsically impossible in the notion that, as years pass, mankind may gain an imaginative insight into some alternative possibility of nature, and may therefore gain understanding of the possibilities of green in other imagined epochs.

There is a rhyme which fits onto the tradition respecting Dr. Whewell, who was Master of Trinity College, Cambridge, about eighty years ago. The rhyme is well-known, and runs thus:

> I am Master of this College;
> And what I know not,
> Is not knowledge.

This attitude is always prevalent in the learned world. It sterilizes imaginative thought, and thereby blocks progress.

In our discussion of understanding, this is the first heresy that I wish to combat. I am not attributing this heresy to Dr. Whewell, although he is said to have exhibited an arrogance, perhaps justified by his very extensive learning. My point is that understanding is never a completed static state of mind. It always bears the character of a process of penetration, incomplete and partial. I fully admit that both aspects of understanding enter into our modes of thought. My thesis is that when we realize ourselves as engaged in a process of penetration, we have a fuller self-knowledge than when we feel a completion of the job of intelligence.

Of course in a sense, there is a completion. But it is a completion presupposing relation to some given undefined environment, imposing a perspective and awaiting exploration. Thus we have a large knowledge of the colour *green*. But this knowledge is limited by the perspective of the present epoch of the universe. It is relevant to a definite unexplored immensity; and this immensity is only itself to be understood by its relevance to alternative immensities.

Shelley, in a chorus of his dramatic poem "Hellas," writes

> Worlds on worlds are rolling ever
> From creation to decay,
> Like the bubbles on a river,
> Sparkling, bursting, borne away.

Amidst this passage of creation, understanding is limited by its finitude. Yet amidst the infinity of things finite, there is nothing finite which is intrinsically denied to it. Such ignorance is accidental; and such possibility of knowledge discloses its relevance to unexplored aspects of things known. Any knowledge of the finite always involves a reference to infinitude.

The specialization which is necessary for the development of civilized thought had in the last century a most unfortunate effect on the philosophic outlook of learned people, and thence on the development of institutions for the promotion of learning. The various departments of universities emphasized their independence of each other. Also a university gained reputation in proportion to its expansion in terms of such subdivision.

As science grew, minds shrank in width of comprehension. The nineteenth century was a period of great achievement, suggestive of an anthill. It failed to produce men of learning with a sensitive appreciation of varieties of interest, of varieties of potentiality. It criticized and exploded, where it should have striven to understand. The detailed setting of its interest is, in every age, a crude mixture of depth of understanding and of triviality of setting, when looked at from beyond that age. And yet to understand the nature of existence, we must grasp the essential character of that depth which, beyond all mistaken details, is the mainspring of the ascent of life discernible in its own age. And here another qualification must be added, namely—If ascent there be.

The very Renaissance itself, of which the last century was the final phase in the agonies of begetting its successor, carried in itself limitations which obstructed the proper expansion of intellectual interest. It was rooted in Greek learning, conceived as the only begetter of civilization. Undoubtedly, the debt of Europe to Greece is beyond words to express. But, after all, Grecian thought, even when expanded into Greek-Hebrew-Egyptian thought, only presents one finite aspect of the many-sided modes of importance which are pressing upon the outskirts of human consciousness.

We must enlarge our effort at understanding. In the nineteenth century, the Greek scholars were somewhat narrower than the best of the Greeks, the Christian scholars were somewhat narrower than the best of the early Popes, and the men of science were somewhat narrower than the founders of the study of mathematics and of physical science. The nineteenth century in the aggregate knew immeasurably more than the Greeks, and the Popes, and the founders of science, all put together. But the moderns had lost the sense of vast alternatives, magnificent or hateful, lurking in the background, and awaiting to overwhelm our safe little traditions. If civilization is to survive, the expansion of understanding is a prime necessity.

2. What is understanding? How can we characterize it? In the first place, understanding always involves the notion of composition. This notion can enter in one of two ways. If the thing understood be composite, the understanding of it can be in reference to its factors, and to their ways of interweaving so as to form that total thing. This mode of comprehension makes evident why the thing is what it is.

The second mode of understanding is to treat the thing

as a unity, whether or not it is capable of analysis, and to obtain evidence as to its capacity for affecting its environment. The first mode may be called the internal understanding, and the second mode is the external understanding.

But this phraseology tells only part of the tale. The two modes are reciprocal: either presupposes the other. The first mode conceives the thing as an outcome, the second mode conceives it as a causal factor. In this latter way of stating our meaning, we have drifted into the notion of understanding the process of the universe. Indeed the presupposition of process seems even to enter into our previous analysis. We can take these ways of explanation of meaning as applying to the understanding of the passage of nature.

It is true that nothing is finally understood until its reference to process has been made evident. And yet, there is the understanding of ideal relationships in abstraction from reference to the passage of brute fact. In the notion of such relationships there is no transition.

For example, throughout mathematics, in one sense, transition does not enter. The interconnections are displayed in their timeless eternity. It is true that the notions of time, and of approach, and of approximation, occur in mathematical discourse. But as used in the science, the timefulness of time and the motion of approach are abstracted from. In mathematics, as understood, the ideal fact stands out self-evident.

There is very little large-scale understanding, even among mathematicians. There are snippets of understanding, and there are snippets of connections between these snippets. These details of connection are also understood. But these fragments of intelligence succeed each other. They do not stand together as one large self-evident coördination. At the best, there is a vague memory of details which have recently been attended to.

This succession of details of self-evidence is termed *proof*. But the large self-evidence of mathematical science is denied to humans.

To give an example, the snippet of knowedge that the addition of 1 and 4 produces the same multiplicity as the addition of 2 and 3, seems to me self-evident. It is a humble bit of knowledge; but, unless I deceive myself, it stands before me with a clarity of insight. I hesitate to claim any such self-evidence when larger numbers are involved. I have recourse to the indignity of proof. Other people have wider powers.

For example, consider Ramanujan, the great Indian mathematician, whose early death was a loss to science analogous to that of Galois. It was said of him that each of the first hundred integers was his personal friend. In other words, his insights of self-evidence, and his delight in such insights, were of the same character as most of us feel for the integers up to the number 5. Personally, I cannot claim intimate friendship beyond that group. Also the restriction of the group somewhat, in my own case, hinders the growth of that feeling of delight which Ramanujan enjoyed.

I confess to a larger pleasure in patterns of relationship in which numerical and quantitative relationships are wholly subordinate. I mention these personal details in order to emphasize the great variety of characters that self-evidence can assume, both as to extent and as to the character of the compositions which are self-evident. The sense of completion, which has already been mentioned, arises from the self-evidence in our understanding. In fact, self-evidence is understanding.

The sense of penetration, which also clings to our experience of intelligibility, has to do with the growth of understanding. To feel the completion apart from any sense of growth, is in fact to fail in understanding. For it is a failure to sense dimly the unexplored relationships with things beyond. To feel the penetration without any sense of completion, is also to fail in understanding. The penetration itself is then deficient in meaning. It lacks achievement.

3. We now come to the notion of "Proof." The thesis that I am developing conceives proof, in the strict sense of that term, as a feeble second-rate procedure. When the word *proof* has been uttered, the next notion to enter the mind is halfheartedness. Unless proof has produced self-evidence and thereby rendered itself unnecessary, it has issued in a second-rate state of mind, producing action devoid of understanding. Self-evidence is the basic fact on which all greatness supports itself. But proof is one of the routes by which self-evidence is often obtained.

As an example of this doctrine, in philosophical writings proof should be at a minimum. The whole effort should be to display the self-evidence of basic truths, concerning the nature of things and their connection. It should be noticed that logical proof starts from premises, and that premises are based upon evidence. Thus evidence is presupposed by logic; at least, it is presupposed by the assumption that logic has any importance.

Philosophy is the attempt to make manifest the fundamental evidence as to the nature of things. Upon the presupposition of this evidence, all understanding rests. A correctly verbalized philosophy mobilizes this basic experience which all premises presuppose. It makes the content of the human mind manageable; it adds meaning to fragmentary details; it discloses disjunctions and conjunctions, consistencies and inconsistencies. Philosophy is the criticism of abstractions which govern special modes of thought.

It follows that philosophy, in any proper sense of the term, cannot be proved. For proof is based upon abstraction. Philosophy is either self-evident, or it is not philosophy. The attempt of any philosophic discourse should be to produce self-evidence. Of course it is impossible to achieve any such aim. But, nonetheless, all inference in philosophy is a sign of that imperfection which clings to all human endeavour. The aim of philosophy is sheer disclosure.

The great difficulty of philosophy is the failure of language. The ordinary intercourse of mankind is concerned with shifting circumstance. It is unnecessary to mention self-evident facts. Thus hunting scenes had been depicted on the walls of caves for thousands of years before the more permanent spatial relations had become a topic for conscious analysis. When the Greeks required terms for the ultimate characters of the actualities of nature, they had to use terms such as water, air, fire, wood.

When the religious thought of the ancient world from Mesopotamia to Palestine, and from Palestine to Egypt, required terms to express that ultimate unity of direction in the universe, upon which all order depends, and which gives its meaning to importance, they could find no way better to express themselves than by borrowing the characteristics of the touchy, vain, imperious tyrants who ruled the empires of the world. In the origin of civilized religion, gods are like dictators. Our modern rituals still retain this taint. The most emphatic repudiations of this archaic notion are to be found scattered in the doctrines of Buddhism and in the Christian Gospels.

Language halts behind intuition. The difficulty of philosophy is the expression of what is self-evident. Our understanding outruns the ordinary usages of words. Philosophy is akin to poetry. Philosophy is the endeavour to find a conventional phraseology for the vivid suggestiveness of the poet. It is the endeavour to reduce Milton's "Lycidas" to prose; and thereby to produce a verbal symbolism manageable for use in other connections of thought.

This reference to philosophy illustrates the fact that understanding is not primarily based on inference. Understanding is self-evidence. But our clarity of intuition is limited, and it flickers. Thus inference enters as means for the attainment of such understanding as we can achieve. Proofs are the tools for the extension of our imperfect self-evidence. They presuppose some clarity; and they also presuppose that this clarity represents an imperfect penetration into our dim recognition of the world around—the world of fact, the world of possibility, the world as valued, the world as purposed.

4. At this point of our discussion another aspect of things claims explicit recognition. It is a general character, whose special forms are termed variously *disorder, evil, error.* In some sense or other, things go wrong; and the notion of correction from worse to better, or the notion of decay from better to worse, enters into our understanding of the nature of things.

It is a temptation for philosophers that they should weave a fairy tale of the adjustment of factors; and then as an appendix introduce the notion of frustration, as a secondary aspect. I suggest to you that this is the criticism to be made on the monistic idealisms of the nineteenth century, and even of the great Spinoza. It is quite incredible that the absolute, as conceived in monistic philosophy, should evolve confusion about its own details.

There is no reason to hold that confusion is less fundamental than is order. Our task is to evolve a general concept which allows room for both; and which also suggests the path for the enlargement of our penetration. My suggestion is that we start from the notion of two aspects of the universe. It includes a factor of unity, involving in its essence the connexity of things, unity of purpose, and unity of enjoyment. The whole notion of importance is referent to this ultimate unity. There is also equally fundamental in the universe, a factor of multiplicity. There are many actualities, each with its own experience, enjoying individually, and yet requiring each other.

Any description of the unity will require the many actualities; and any description of the many will require the notion of the unity from which importance and purpose is derived. By reason of the essential individuality of the many things, there are conflicts of finite realizations. Thus the summation of the many into the one, and the derivation of importance from the one into the many, involves the notion of disorder, of conflict, of frustration.

These are the primary aspects of the universe which common sense brooding over the aspects of existence hands over to philosophy for elucidation into some coherence of understanding. Philosophy shirks its task when it summarily dismisses one side of the dilemma. We can never fully understand. But we can increase our penetration.

When there is a full understanding, any particular item belongs to what is already clear. Thus it is merely a repetition of the known. In that sense, there is tautology. Thus tautology is the intellectual amusement of the Infinite.

Also in the same sense, the selection of the particular item for emphasis is equally arbitrary. It is the convention by means of which the Infinite governs its concentration of attention.

For the finite individual there is penetration to novelty in its own experience; and the selection of detail is subject to the causation from which that individual originates.

Philosophy tends to oscillate between the points of view belonging to the infinite and to the finite. Thus understanding, however imperfect, is the self-evidence of pattern, so far as it has been discriminated. Also for the finite experience, inference is the achievement of further penetration into such self-evidence.

A partially understood pattern is more definite as to what it excludes than as to what its completion would include. As to inclusion there are an infinitude of alternative modes of completion. But so far as there is any definiteness attaching to the incomplete disclosure, certain factors are definitely excluded. The foundation of logic upon the notion of inconsistency was first discovered and developed by Professor Henry Sheffer of Harvard, about twenty years ago. Professor Sheffer also emphasized the notion of pattern, as fundamental to logic. In this way, one of the great advances in mathematical logic was accomplished.

In the first place, by basing logic upon the concept of inconsistency, the notion of the finite is definitely introduced. For as Spinoza pointed out, the finite is that which excludes other things comparable to itself. Thus inconsistency bases logic upon Spinoza's concept of finitude.

In the second place, as Sheffer pointed out, the notions of negation and of inference can be derived from that of inconsistency. Thus the whole movement of logic is provided for. We may notice that this basis for logic suggests that the notion of frustration is more akin to finite mentality; while the notion of harmonious conjunction is derived from the concept of a monistic universe. It is for philosophy to coördinate the two aspects which the world presents.

In the third place, this basis for logic enlightens our understanding of process, which is a fundamental fact in our experience. We are in the present; the present is always shifting; it is derived from the past; it is shaping the future;

it is passing into the future. This is process, and in the universe it is an inexorable fact.

5. But if all things can be together, why should there be process? One answer to this question embodies a denial of process. According to this answer process is mere appearance, devoid of significance for ultimate reality. This solution seems to me to be very inadequate. How can the unchanging unity of fact generate the delusion of change? Surely, the satisfactory answer must embody an understanding of the interweaving of change and permanence, each required by the other. This interweaving is a primary fact of experience. It is at the base of our concepts of personal identity, of social identity, and of all sociological functionings.

Meanwhile, another aspect of the relationship between inconsistency and process must now occupy us. Inconsistency is the fact that the two states of things which constitute the respective meanings of a pair of propositions cannot exist together. It denies a possible conjunction between these meanings. But these meanings have been brought together in the very judgment of inconsistency. This is the sort of perplexity that Plato alluded to, when he makes one of his characters say, "Not-being is a sort of being."

The conclusion that I draw is that the word *together,* and indeed all words expressive of conjunction in general, without definite specification, are very ambiguous. For example, the little word *and* is a nest of ambiguity. It is very astounding how slight has been the analysis of the ambiguities of words expressive of conjunctions. Such words are the death-traps for accuracy of reasoning. Unfortunately, they occur abundantly in sentences, expressed in the most perfect literary form. Thus an admirable literary style is no security for logical consistency.

In reading philosophic literature every word expressive of conjunction must be deeply pondered over. If it be used twice in the same sentence, or in neighbouring sentences, can we be sure that the two usages embody the same meaning, at least sufficiently for the purposes of the argument?

I suggest to you that the contradictions, famous in ancient and in modern logic, arise from such ambiguities. Many words which are not formally conjunctions, are expressive of a conjunctive meaning. For example, the word *class* has all the manifold ambiguity of the word *and*. The understanding of pattern, and of the conjunctions involved in various patterns, depends upon the study of such ambiguities. On this topic philosophic literature is very simple-minded. So many vigorous and cogent arguments fall into this trap.

We must now return to the topic of inconsistency and process. The concept that two propositions, which we will name *p* and *q*, are inconsistent, must mean that in the modes of togetherness illustrated in some presupposed environment the meanings of the propositions *p* and *q* cannot both occur. Neither meaning may occur or either may occur, but not both. Now process is the way by which the universe escapes from the exclusions of inconsistency.

Such exclusions belong to the finitude of circumstance. By means of process, the universe escapes from the limitations of the finite. Process is the immanence of the infinite in the finite; whereby all bounds are burst, and all inconsistencies dissolved.

No specific finitude is an ultimate shackle upon the universe. In process the finite possibilities of the universe travel towards their infinitude of realization.

In the nature of things there are no ultimate exclusions, expressive in logical terms. For if we extend the stretch of our attention throughout the passage of time, two entities which are inconsistent for occurrence on this planet during a certain day in the long past and are inconsistent during another day in more recent past—these two entities may be consistent when we embrace the whole period involved, one entity occurring during the earlier day, and the other during the later day. Thus inconsistency is relative to the abstraction involved.

An easy intellectual consistency can be attained, provided that we rest content with high abstraction. Pure mathematics is the chief example of success by adherence to such rigid abstraction. Again, the importance of mathematics, as finally disclosed in the sixteenth and seventeenth centuries, illustrates the doctrine that the advance of the finite human understanding requires the adherence to some judicious abstraction, and the development of thought within that abstraction. The disclosure of this method has issued in the progressive science of modern civilization, within the last three thousand years.

6. But the discovery has been gradual, and the method is even now imperfectly understood. Learned people have handled the specialization of thought with an incredible lack of precaution. It is almost universally assumed that the growth of a specialism leaves unaffected the presuppositions as to the perspective of the environment which were sufficient for the initial stages. It cannot be too clearly understood that the expansion of any special topic changes its whole meaning from top to bottom. As the subject matter of a science expands, its relevance to the universe contracts. For it presupposes a more strictly defined environment.

The definition of the environment is exactly what is omitted from special abstraction. Such definition is an irrelevance. It is irrelevant because it requires an understanding of the infinitude of things. It is therefore impossible. All that we can do is to make an abstraction, to presuppose that it is relevant, and to push ahead within that presupposition.

This sharp division between the clarity of finite science and the dark universe beyond is itself an abstraction from concrete fact. For example, we can explore our presuppositions. Take the special case of natural science, we presuppose geometry. But what sort of geometry? There are many kinds. In fact, there are an indefinite number of alternative geometries. Which one are we to choose?

We all know that this is a topic which has bothered, or elated, physical science during the last thirty years. At last the great scientists are coming to conclusions which we will all accept. And yet a sceptical doubt intrudes. How do we know that only one geometry is relevant to the complex happenings of nature? Perhaps a three-dimensional geometry is relevant to one sort of occurrences; and a fifteen-dimensional geometry is required for another sort.

Of course our more obvious sense perceptions seem to clamour for three dimensions, especially sight. On the other hand sound, though voluminous, is very vague as to the dimensions of its volumes, as between three or fifteen, for instance. Also any change in scale, to the very small or to the very large, makes surprising changes in the characters of the happenings disclosed so far as we can observe.

We have developed very special types of sensory observation; and in consequence we are wedded to a correspondingly special set of results, true enough if we introduce the proper limitations. But as our science expands the area of relationship to other aspects of nature becomes increasingly important.

Perhaps our knowledge is distorted unless we can comprehend its essential connection with happenings which involve spatial relationships of fifteen dimensions. The dogmatic assumption of the trinity of nature as its sole important dimensional aspect has been useful in the past. It is becoming dangerous in the present. In the future it may be a fatal barrier to the advance of knowledge.

Also, this planet, or this nebula in which our sun is placed, may be gradually advancing towards a change in the general character of its spatial relations. Perhaps in the dim future mankind, if it then exists, will look back to the queer, contracted three-dimensional universe from which the nobler, wider existence has emerged.

These speculations are, at present, neither proved nor disproved. They have however a mythical value. They do represent how concentration on coherent verbalizations of certain aspects of human experience may block the advance of understanding. Too many apples from the tree of systematized knowledge lead to the fall of progress.

The sense of advance, of penetration, is essential to sustain interest. Also there are two types of advance. One is the advance in the use of assigned patterns for the coördination of an increased variety of detail.

But the assignment of the type of pattern restricts the choice of details. In this way the infinitude of the universe is dismissed as irrelevant. The advance which has started with the freshness of sunrise degenerates into a dull accumulation of minor feats of coördination. The history of thought and the history of art illustrate this doctrine. We cannot prescribe the pattern of progress.

It is true that advance is partly the gathering of details into assigned patterns. This is the safe advance of dogmatic spirits, fearful of folly. But history discloses another type of progress, namely the introduction of novelty of pattern into conceptual experience. In this way, details hitherto undiscriminated or dismissed as casual irrelevances are lifted into coördinated experience. There is a new vision of the great Beyond.

7. Thus understanding has two modes of advance, the

gathering of detail within assigned pattern, and the discovery of novel pattern with its emphasis on novel detail. The intelligence of mankind has been halted by dogmatism as to pattern of connection. Religious thought, aesthetic thought, the understanding of social structures, the scientific analysis of observation, have alike been dwarfed by this fatal virus.

It entered European thought at the very beginning of its brilliant foundation. Epicurus, Plato, Aristotle, were alike convinced of the certainty of various elements in their experience, in the exact forms in which they understood them. They were unaware of the perils of abstraction. Later on, in his *Critique of Pure Reason,* Kant gave a masterly exposition of the reasons why we should be so certain. There was a concurrence of genius as to this certainty.

It is a tragedy of history, that in the sense in which these great men held these beliefs, not one of their doctrines has survived the wider knowledge of the last two centuries. Mathematics is not true in the sense in which Plato conceived it. Sense data are not clear, distinct, and primary, in the sense in which Epicurus believed.

The history of thought is a tragic mixture of vibrant disclosure and of deadening closure. The sense of penetration is lost in the certainty of completed knowledge. This dogmatism is the antichrist of learning.

In the full concrete connection of things, the characters of the things connected enter into the character of the connectivity which joins them.

Every example of friendship exhibits the particular characters of the two friends. Two other people are inconsistent in respect to that completely defined friendship. Again the colours in a picture form a composition, which is partly geometrical If we merely consider the abstract

58

geometrical relationship, a patch of red can be substituted for a patch of blue. In this geometrical abstraction the red is just as consistent with the remaining patches of colours as was the blue. But if we consider the picture more concretely, perhaps a masterpiece has been ruined. The red is inconsistent with the concrete effect on the composition produced by the blue.

Thus in proportion as we penetrate towards concrete apprehension, inconsistency rules. Namely, all entities, except one, are inconsistent with the production of the particular effect which the one entity would produce. In proportion to our relapse towards abstraction, many entities will alternatively produce the same abstract effect. Thus consistency grows with abstraction from the concrete.

There is thus an ambiguity in the notion of inconsistency. There is the sheer difference produced by the distinction between entities. If the patch be scarlet, it cannot also be pale blue. The two notions are inconsistent by reason of the sheer distinction between red and blue, in that they are distinct colours. There is also the distinction in aesthetic enjoyment. The blue may be a factor in a picture which is a masterpiece, while the substitution of red in the same geometrical position destroys the whole aesthetic value. On the other hand, if interest be wholly directed to the geometrical relationships, red or blue may do equally well to mark out that area.

We should now understand that there are two types of inconsistency. These may be termed respectively, the logical type, and the aesthetic type. The logical type is based on the difference between different things, conceived as alternative factors in a composition. It cannot be indifferent to the totality of a composition, as to which of two distinct things fill an assigned role in the pattern of that composite entity. The difference in the factors will produce different compositions. Also the addition of factors disrupts the underlying presuppositions.

We can never understand a composition in its full concrete effectiveness for all possibilities of environment. We are aware only of an abstraction. For this abstraction the change or addition of factors may be indifferent. There is always a nemesis hanging over the equivalence, or consistency, of different things. As we enlarge self-evidence the abstraction shrinks, and our understanding penetrates towards the concrete fact. Thus, sooner or later, growth in knowledge leads to the evidence of antagonism involved in difference.

8. The doctrine of understanding, as developed in this lecture, applies beyond logic. The aesthetic experience is another mode of the enjoyment of self-evidence. This conclusion is as old as European thought. The relation of the mathematical doctrine of proportion in its application to music and to architecture excited interest in the Pythagorean and Platonic schools. Also the feeling, widespread among mathematicians, that some proofs are more beautiful than others, should excite the attention of philosophers.

I suggest to you that the analogy between aesthetics and logic is one of the undeveloped topics of philosophy.

In the first place, they are both concerned with the enjoyment of a composition, as derived from the interconnections of its factors. There is one whole, arising from the interplay of many details. The importance arises from the vivid grasp of the interdependence of the one and the many. If either side of this antithesis sinks into the background, there is trivialization of experience, logical and aesthetic.

The distinction between logic and aesthetics consists in the degree of abstraction involved. Logic concentrates attention upon high abstraction, and aesthetics keeps as close to the concrete as the necessities of finite understanding permit. Thus logic and aesthetics are at the two extremes of the dilemma of the finite mentality in its partial penetration of the infinite.

Either of these topics can be considered from two points of view. There is the discovery of a logical complex, and the enjoyment of that complex when discovered. Also there is the construction of an aesthetic composition, and the enjoyment of that composition when composed. This distinction between creation and enjoyment must not be overstressed. But it is there; and the close of this lecture is concerned with the enjoyment and not with creation.

The characteristic attitude of logical understanding is to start with the details, and to pass to the construction achieved. Logical enjoyment passes from the many to the one. The characters of the many are understood as permitting that unity of construction.

Logic employs symbols; but only as symbols. For example, the difference in the spacing of the lines, in the width of the margin, in the size of the page—octavo, or quarto, or duodecimo, has not as yet entered into the symbolism.

The understanding of logic is the enjoyment of the abstracted details as permitting that abstract unity. As the enjoyment develops, the revelation is the unity of the construct. We are facing a possibility for the universe, namely how the abstract in its own nature harbours that approach to concretion. Logic starts with primitive ideas, and puts them together.

The movement of aesthetic enjoyment is in the opposite direction. We are overwhelmed by the beauty of the building, by the delight of the picture, by the exquisite balance of the sentence. The whole precedes the details.

We then pass to discrimination. As in a moment, the

details force themselves upon us as the reasons for the totality of the effect. In aesthetics, there is a totality disclosing its component parts.

In the history of European thought, the discussion of aesthetics has been almost ruined by the emphasis upon the harmony of the details. The enjoyment of Greek art is always haunted by a longing for the details to exhibit some rugged independence apart from the oppressive harmony.

In the greatest examples of any form of art, a miraculous balance is achieved. The whole displays its component parts, each with its own value enhanced; and the parts lead up to a whole, which is beyond themselves, and yet not destructive of themselves. It is however remarkable how often the preliminary studies of the details—if preserved —are more interesting than the final details as they appear in the complete work. Even the greatest works of art fall short of perfection.

By reason of the greater concreteness of the aesthetic experience, it is a wider topic than that of the logical experience. Indeed, when the topic of aesthetics has been sufficiently explored, it is doubtful whether there will be anything left over for discussion. But this doubt is unjustified. For the essence of great experience is penetration into the unknown, the unexperienced.

Both logic and aesthetics concentrate on the closed fact. Our lives are passed in the experience of disclosure. As we lose this sense of disclosure, we are shedding that mode of functioning which is the soul. We are descending to mere conformity with the average of the past. Complete conformity means the loss of life. There remains the barren existence of inorganic nature.

In the three lectures now concluded, the assemblage of these ideas, most fundamental for philosophic thought, has been attempted. The systematization has been of the slightest; and under the guise of three headings a variety of notions has been introduced.

There is one moral to be drawn. Apart from detail, and apart from system, a philosophic outlook is the very foundation of thought and of life. The sort of ideas we attend to, and the sort of ideas which we push into the negligible background, govern our hopes, our fears, our control of behaviour. As we think, we live. This is why the assemblage of philosophic ideas is more than a specialist study. It moulds our type of civilization.

Perspective

There is reason to believe that human genius reached its culmination in the twelve hundred years preceding and including the initiation of the Christian Epoch. Within that period the main concepts of aesthetic experience, of religion, of humane social relations, of political wisdom, of mathematical deduction, and of observational science, were developed and discussed. Of course, each one of these aspects of civilization has an immensely longer history, stretching back to the animals. But within that period, the achievements of mankind attained an amplitude of effectiveness. Also their relevance to the ideals of human life was consciously entertained. In the earlier stages of this period, the Homeric poems and various Confuscian modes of thought emerged, and in the final stage, Virgil, the Gospel of St. John, and the political structure of the Roman Empire.

The techniques of life flourished. The initiation of each was earlier than this period. For example, the technique of writing gradually developed through many ages. But its facility of use so as to be a medium for the preservation of intimate thoughts of individual people belongs to this epoch. Antecedently to this period it recorded the orders of kings and the boasts of conquerors. Analogous considerations apply to the development of metals, of horses, of roads, of navigation: civilization was in its infancy. Within the period we find achievement. Of course, since then, there has been progress in knowledge and technique. But it has been along the path laid down by the activities of that golden age. The history of Europe during the past eighteen hundred years is the sequel.

One unfortunate result of this derivation from a brilliant past has been that defective insights of the earlier period have been rooted in language and literature. Also language dictates our unconscious presuppositions of thought.

For example, single words, each with its dictionary meaning, and single sentences, each bounded by full stops, suggest the possibility of complete abstraction from any environment. Thus the problem of philosophy is apt to be conceived as the understanding of the interconnections of things, each understandable, apart from reference to anything else.

2. This presupposition is erroneous. Let us dismiss it, and assume that each entity, of whatever type, essentially involves its own connection with the universe of other things. This connection can be viewed as being what the universe is for that entity either in the way of accomplishment or in the way of potentiality. It can be termed the perspective of the universe for that entity. For example, these are the perspectives of the universe for the number three, and for the colour blue, and for any one definite occasion of realized fact.

Each perspective for any one qualitative abstraction such as a number, or a colour, involves an infinitude of alternative potentialities. On the other hand, the perspective for a factual occasion involves the elimination of alternatives in respect to the matter-of-fact realization involved in that present occasion, and the reduction of alternatives as to the future; since that occasion, as a member of its own contemporary world, is one of the factors conditioning the future beyond itself.

This question of the meanings of our current abstractions of all types of entities is more than a metaphysical puzzle for learned people. It is a question of practical good sense in our everyday judgments of affairs. Our danger is to take notions which are valid for one perspective of the universe involved in one group of events and to apply them uncritically to other events involving some discrepancy of perspective. A correction is wanted by reason of this discrepancy. In the three lectures of this second Part, I shall be discussing various applications of this doctrine of the perspective involved in every entity. Also it will be necessary to refer to the misconceptions which arise from its neglect.

This notion of perspectives of the universe is discussed in my *Science and The Modern World,* under the heading "Relational Essence." But in that discussion the perspectives of qualitative entities are alone considered. Here the notion has been broadened.

3. The most simple doctrine about types of being is that some extreme type exists independently of the rest of things. For example, Greek philosophers, and in particular Plato, seem to have held this doctrine in respect to qualitative abstractions, such as number, geometrical relations, moral characteristics, and the qualitative disclosures of the higher sense perceptions. Namely, according to this tradition in so far as we abstract from our experience the brute particularity of happening here, and now, amid this envi-

ronment, there remains a residue with self-identities, differences, and essential interconnections, which seems to have no essential reference to the passage of events. According to this doctrine, as the result of this discard of the factor of transition we rivet our attention on the eternal realm of forms. In this imagined realm there is no passage, no loss, no gain. It is complete in itself. It is self-sustaining. It is therefore the realm of the "completely real."

This is the notion that has haunted philosophy. It was never far from Greek thought. Later, it transformed the Hebraic elements in Christian Theology.

We must admit that in some sense or other, we inevitably presuppose this realm of forms, in abstraction from passage, loss, and gain. For example, the multiplication table up to "twelve-times-twelve" is a humble member of it. In all our thoughts of what has happened and can happen, we presuppose the multiplication table as essentially qualifying the course of history, whenever it is relevant. It is always at hand, and there is no escape. So far as our vision is clear, there is that element of certain knowledge. But, how clear is our vision?

This notion of the realm of timeless forms leads to rhetorical, question-begging phrases, such as "self-sustaining," "completely-real," "perfection," "certainty."

Let us take these phrases in reverse order. We make mistakes in arithmetic. We can misconceive the very meaning of number and of the interconnections of number. The great mathematicians of the seventeenth and eighteenth centuries misconceived the subject matter of their studies. For example, in respect to the notions of infinitesimals, of the necessary precautions in the use of infinite series, and the doctrine of complex numbers, their discoveries were suffused with error.

The notion of a sphere of human knowledge characterized by unalloyed truth is the pet delusion of dogmatists, whether they be theologians, scientists, or humanistic scholars.

Again, perfection is a notion which haunts human imagination. It cannot be ignored. But its naïve attachment to the realm of forms is entirely without justification. How about the form of mud, and the forms of evil, and other forms of imperfection? In the house of forms, there are many mansions.

Finally, consider together the two notions, self-sustaining and complete reality. Every form in its very nature refers to some sort of realization. The numerical notions, such as "five" and "six," refer to concepts of things which may exemplify them. The notion of the numbers up to six, as existing in a vacuum is idiotic. The muddiness is referent to mud, and forms of evil require evil things, in some sense or other.

Thus the forms are essentially referent beyond themselves. It is mere phantasy to impute to them any "absolute reality," which is devoid of implications beyond itself. The realm of forms is the realm of potentiality, and the very notion of potentiality has an external meaning. It refers to life and motion. It refers to inclusion and exclusion. It refers to hope, fear, and intention. Phrasing this statement more generally,—it refers to appetition. It refers to the development of actuality, which realizes form and is yet more than form. It refers to past, present, and future.

Again everything is something, which in its own way is real. When you refer to something as unreal, you are merely conceiving a type of reality to which that "something" does not belong. But to be real is not to be self-sustaining. Also modes of reality require each other. It is the task of philosophy to elucidate the relevance to each other of various types of existence. We cannot exhaust such types because there are an unending number of them. But we can start with two types which to us seen as extremes; and can then discern these types as requiring other types to express their mutual relevance to each other.

I do not affirm that these two types are fundamentally more ultimate, or more simple, than other derivative types. But I do maintain that for human experience, they are natural starting points for the understanding of types of existence.

The two types in question can be named respectively, "The Type of Actuality," and "The Type of Pure Potentiality."

These types require each other, namely actuality is the exemplification of potentiality, and potentiality is the characterization of actuality, either in fact or in concept.

Also the interconnections of the two extreme types involve the introduction of other types, namely type upon type, each type expressing some mode of composition. I suggest to you that the traditions of linguistic expression are singularly naïve in the handling of modes of composition. Some blessed word, such as the word *composition* itself, covers up all the perplexities that reflection discloses.

At this point we had better ask ourselves, What are we appealing to in the development of philosophic thought? Where is the evidence?

The answer is evidently human experience, as shared by civilized intercommunication. The expression of such evidence, so far as it is widely shared, is to be found in law, in moral and sociological habits, in literature and art as ministering to human satisfactions, in historical judgments on the rise and decay of social systems, and in science. It is also diffused throughout the meanings of words and linguistic expressions.

Philosophy is a secondary activity. It meditates on this variety of expression. It finds types of things, each type exemplifying a mode of existence, with its own characteristic reality. Also all its sources of information express various aspects of the interfusion of things. Thus the task of philosophy is the understanding of the interfusion of modes of existence.

There is also one final consideration, namely that philosophy is limited in its sources to the world as disclosed in human experience.

4. With this interlude recalling our evidence, we return to the question, What is the meaning of actuality conceived as the extreme contrast to potentiality? We recur to the statement: actuality and potentiality require each other in the reciprocal roles of example and character. Thus in order to understand actuality, we must ask, what is character, and what is it that has character?

To the latter half of this question many answers have been given, each answer referent to some important aspect of human experience. They can be grouped under three titles, namely, "Substances," "Happenings," "The Absolute." But these titles refer to the discussions of the learned world prolonged through centuries of civilization. They are important, though they are far from naïve experience.

Our more direct experience groups itself into two large divisions, each capable of further analysis. One division is formed by the sense of qualitative experience derived from antecedent fact, enjoyed in the personal unity of present fact, and conditioning future fact. In this division of experience, there are the sense of derivation from without, the sense of immediate enjoyment within, and the sense of transmission beyond. This complex sense of enjoyment involves the past, the present, the future. It is at once complex, vague, and imperative. It is the realization of our essential connection with the world without, and also of our own individual existence now. It carries with it the placing of our immediate experience as a fact in history, derivative, actual, and effective. It also carries with it the sense of immediate experience as the essence of an individual fact with its own qualities. The main characteristic of such experience is complexity, vagueness, and compulsive intensity. In one respect the vagueness yields a comparatively sharp cut division, namely, the differentiation of the world into the animal body which is the region of intimate, intense, mutual expression, and the rest of nature where the intimacy and intensity of feeling fails to penetrate. My brain, my heart, my bowels, my lungs, are mine, with an intimacy of mutual adjustment. The sunrise is a message from the world beyond such directness of relation. The behaviour system of the body has an element of direct relationship with the transitions of quality in personal experience. This directness is lacking in the relationship of the external world to the flux of feeling. For this reason psychology and physiology are difficult to dissociate from each other, either for the purposes of abstract science or for the purposes of the medical practitioner. The behaviour systems of the human body and of intimate experience are closely entangled.

5. The second division of human experience has a character very different from the first division of bodily feelings. It lacks the intimacy, the intensity, and the vagueness. It consists of the discrimination of forms as expressing external natural facts in their relationship to the body. Let this division be termed *sense perception*.

Now sense perception belongs to the higher animals. We will consider it as we know it; that is to say, as in human experience. It is a sophisticated derivative from the more primitive bodily experience which constituted the division of experience first considered. But it has outgrown its origin, and has inverted every emphasis. Its primary characteristic is clarity, distinctness, and indifference. Its emotional effects are secondary derivatives, achieved by awakening reactions other than itself. This is Hume's doctrine. Only Hume neglected the primary experiences of bodily intimacy; although he used these primary experiences in describing our reactions to sense perceptions.

In sense perception we discern the external world with its various parts characterized by form of quality, and interrelated by forms which express both separation and connection. These forms of quality are the sensa, such as shades of blue, and tones of sound. The forms expressing distinction and connection are the spatial and temporal forms. The world, as interpreted by exclusive attention to such forms of sense perception, I will term *nature*.

These forms, qualitative and spatio-temporal, dominate this experience. They are indifferent to emotion, being just themselves, namely the vivid realization of things capable of abstraction from that instance of actuality with its cargo of emotion. Nature is devoid of impulse.

Sense perception is the triumph of abstraction in animal experience. Such abstraction arises from the growth of selective emphasis. It endows human life with three gifts, namely, an approach to accuracy, a sense of the qualitative differentiation of external activities, a neglect of essential connections.

These three characters of the higher animal experience —namely, approximate accuracy, qualitative assignment, essential omission—together constitute the focus of consciousness, as in human experience.

Aristotelian logic is founded on this primary deliverance of abstractive consciousness, namely, "that entity exemplifying this quality, apart from any reference to things beyond."

Also scientific practice is founded upon the same characteristic of omission. In order to observe accurately, concentrate on that observation, dismissing from consciousness all irrelevant modes of experience. But there is no irrelevance. Thus the whole of science is based upon neglected modes of relevance, which nevertheless dominate the social group entertaining those scientific modes of thought. For this reason the progress of systematized knowledge has a double aspect. There is progress in the discovery of the intricacies of composition which that system admits. There is also progress in the discovery of the limitations of the system in its omission to indicate its dependence upon environmental coördinations of modes of existence which have essential relevance to the entities within the system. Since all things are connected, any system which omits some things must necessarily suffer from such limitations.

The emphasis upon the higher sense percepta, such as sights and sounds, has damaged the philosophic development of the preceding two centuries. The question, What *do* we know?, has been transformed into the question, What *can* we know? This latter question has been dogmatically solved by the presupposition that all knowledge starts from the consciousness of spatio-temporal patterns of such sense percepta.

6. The study of human knowledge should start with a survey of the vague variety, discernible in the transitions of human experience. It cannot safely base itself upon simple arbitrary assumptions, such as this assumption of spatio-temporal patterns of sensa as the source of all knowledge. There is something very special about such spatio-

temporal patterns, and also about arithmetic patterns. Speaking from my own frame of mind, I revolt against this concentration upon the multiplication table and the regular solids: in other words, against the notion that topology, based upon numerical relations, contains in itself the one fundamental key to the understanding of the nature of things. Surely we should start from principles which are larger, more penetrating. Arithmetic and topology are specialties.

What are the general principles of division which dominate that creative process which we term our lives? We can only appeal to our direct insight—to what Descartes termed, our *inspectio*. Our judgment, that is, our judicium to which Descartes also appealed, requires an inspection to provide the material from which decision arises. The question therefore is as to those fundamental modes dominating experience. Such modes are modes of division, each division involving differences with essential contrasts.

I suggest to you as fundamental characterizations of our experience, three principles of division expressed by the three pairs of opposites—"Clarity and Vagueness," "Order and Disorder," "The Good and the Bad." Our endeavour to understand creation should start from these modes of experience.

There is a natural affinity between order and goodness. It is not usual to accuse people of "orderly conduct." Undoubtedly there are limits to the excellence of mere order. It can be overdone. But there can be no excellence except upon some basis of order. Mere disorder results in a nonentity of achievement. It is one purpose of this lecture to examine this affinity between order and goodness, and to note its limitations.

This is an ambitious aim, when we remember that the most famous lecture in the whole history of European thought was devoted to this topic. It was delivered nearly two thousand three hundred years ago. The title of this lecture did not allude to order. But we do know that the subject matter was largely concerned with mathematics. It is worth considering, from our own point of view today, why Plato naturally thought of mathematics when he sat down to write a lecture on "The Good." We are not concerned with the precise mathematical doctrines which were enunciated in that lecture, nor even with the precise relation of mathematics to the forms as conceived, or misconceived, by Plato. My topic is the relation of order to the good, and the relation of mathematics to the notion of order.

At first sight, the notion of any important connection between the multiplication table and the moral beauty of the Sermon on the Mount is fantastic. And yet, consideration of the development of human clarity of experience from its foundation of confused animal satisfactions discloses mathematical understanding as the primary example of insight into the nature of the good. Also we must remember that morals constitute only one aspect of the good, an aspect often overstressed.

The animals enjoy structure. They can build nests and dams: they can follow the trail of scent through the forest. The concrete realized facts, confused and intermixed, dominate animal life. Man understands structure. He abstracts its dominating principle from the welter of detail. He can imagine alternative illustration. He constructs distant objectives. He can compare the variety of issues. He can aim at the best. But the essence of this human control of purposes depends on the understanding of structure in its variety of applications.

To be human requires the study of structure. To be animal merely requires its enjoyment. An animal enjoys social relations; a human being has the capacity to know the exact number of individuals involved in such social relations, and also can conceive the exact relevance of number to enjoyment. In other words, in the passage from our lower type of animal experience to our higher type of human experience, we have acquired a selective emphasis whereby the finite occasions of experience receive clear definition.

This clarity of human vision both enhances the uniqueness of each individual occasion, and at the same time discloses its essential relationships to occasions other than itself. It emphasizes both finite individuality and also to relationship to other individualities.

Further, it discloses some analysis of the matter-of-fact in immediate realization. And yet, by this disclosure it brings into prominence the potentialities for alternative realizations, in the past, in the future, in the present. It tells what may be, and what may have been. It lays bare diversities and analogies. Mankind enjoys a vision of the function of form within fact, and of the issue of value from this interplay. That day in the history of mankind when the vague appreciation of multitude was transformed into the exact observation of number, human beings made a long stride in the comprehension of that interweaving of form necessary for the higher life which is the disclosure of the good.

I remember an incident proving that at least some squirrels have not crossed this borderline of civilization. We were in a charming camp situated amidst woodland bordering a Vermont lake. A squirrel had made its nest in our main sitting room, placing it in a hole in brickwork around the fireplace. She came in and out to her young ones, ignoring the presence of the human family. One day, she decided that her family had grown up beyond the nursery stage. So, one by one, she carried them out to the edge of the woodland. As I remember across the years, there were three children. But when the mother had placed them on the rock outside, the family group looked to her very different from its grouping within the nest. She was vaguely disturbed, and ran backwards and forwards two or three times to make quite sure that no young squirrel had been left behind. She was unable to count, nor had she identified them by christening them with names. All she knew was that the vague multitude on the rock seemed very unlike the vague multitude in the nest. Her family experiences lacked the perception of the exact limitation imposed by number. As a result she was mildly and vaguely disturbed. If the mother could have counted, she would have experienced the determinate satisfaction of a job well-done in the rearing of three children; or, in the case of loss, she would have suffered vivid pain from the absence of a determinate child. But she lacked adequate experience of any precise form of limitation.

Thus the rise in vivid experience of the good and of the bad depends upon the intuition of exact forms of limitation. Among such forms number has a chief place.

7. In the discussion of our deeper experiences, religious and mystic, an unbalanced emphasis has been placed upon the mere sense of infinitude. Any being, overwhelmed with this sense, would rank lower than the squirrel. All forms of realization express some aspect of finitude. Such a form expresses its nature as being *this,* and not *that.* In other words, it expresses exclusion; and exclusion means finitude.

The full solemnity of the world arises from the sense of positive achievement within the finite, combined with the sense of modes of infinitude stretching beyond each finite fact. This infinitude is required by each fact to express its necessary relevance beyond its own limitations. It expresses a perspective of the universe.

Importance arises from this fusion of the finite and the infinite. The cry, "Let us eat and drink, for tomorrow we die," expresses the triviality of the merely finite. The mystic, ineffective slumber expresses the vacuity of the merely infinite. Those theologians do religion a bad service who emphasize infinitude at the expense of the finite transitions within history. With the foregoing discussion in mind, we recur to the three pairs of opposites: clarity and vagueness, order and disorder, the good and the bad. It is natural to associate clarity and order with the attainment of the good; and to associate vagueness and disorder with the bad. For example, in writing a testimonial, the phrase "Her mind is clear and orderly" would be taken as praise; while the phrase "Her mind is vague and disorderly" would be read as condemnation. The reason for such judgment is based upon the fact that clarity and orderliness enable the possessor to deal with foreseen situations. They are necessary foundations for the maintenance of existing social situations. And yet they are not enough. Transcendence of mere clarity and order is necessary for dealing with the unforeseen, for progress, for excitement. Life degenerates when enclosed within the shackles of mere conformation. A power of incorporating vague and disorderly elements of experience is essential for the advance into novelty.

The understanding of the universe is rooted in the implications of this advance. Apart from it, creation is meaningless, divorced from change. Time has then no application to the static nature of things. Existence is meaningless. The universe is reduced to static futility—devoid of life and motion.

In the history of European philosophic thought, in the history of great thinkers, a curious wavering can be detected on this question. The appeal to life and motion is interwoven with the presupposition of the supreme reality as devoid of change. Changeless order is conceived as the final perfection, with the result that the historic universe is degraded to a status of partial reality, issuing into the notion of mere appearance. The result has been that the most evident characteristic of our experience has been dismissed into a subordinate role in metaphysical construction. We live in a world of turmoil. Philosophy, and religion, as influenced by orthodox philosophic thought, dismiss turmoil. Such dismissal is the outcome of tired decadence. We should beware of philosophies which express the dominant emotions of periods of slow social decay. Our inheritance of philosophic thought is infected with the decline and fall of the Roman Empire, and with the decadence of eastern civilizations. It expresses the exhaustion following upon the first three thousand years of advancing civilization. A better balance is required. For civilizations rise as well as fall. We require philosophy to explain the rise of types of order, the transitions from type to type, and the mixtures of good and bad involved in the universe as it stands self-evident in our experience. Such a universe is the locus of importance. A frozen, motionless universe can at most be the topic of pure knowledge, with the bare comment—That is so.

Emphasis limited to special aspects of things explicitly experienced has advanced science, and has hampered philosophy. Consider for example the effect on European thought of the rise of mathematical science, about four centuries before the Christian Era. Mathematics was concerned with notions which at that time introduced no sense either of transition or of creation. Numbers and geometrical forms constituted the sole content of Greek mathematics.

It is unnecessary to dwell on the importance of the science of these special mathematical forms. It has transformed civilization. But its effect on Greek thought was very mixed. As the Greeks understood that science, the notion of transition was in the background. Each number, each ratio, each geometric form exhibited a static attainment. The number *twelve* (in their conception of it) had no reference to creation; neither had the ratio *six to two;* neither had the geometric form of the circle. These ideal forms are for them motionless, impervious, and self-sufficient—each representing a perfection peculiar to itself. Such was the reaction of Greek thought to the fundamental notions of mathematics. The human mind was dazzled by this glimpse of eternity. The result of this revelation was that Greek philosophy—at least in its most influential school—conceived ultimate reality in the guise of static existences with timeless interrelations. Perfection was unrelated to transition. Creation, with its world in change, was an inferior avocation of a static absolute.

8. The effect on subsequent European thought of this impulse from the golden age of Greece has been threefold. In the first place, the static absolute has been passed over to philosophic theology, as a primary presupposition.

In the second place, the abstractions of structure, such as mathematical notions and all notions involving ways of composition, have been endowed with an eminent reality, apart from individual compositions in which they occur.

In the third place, these abstractions of structure have been conceived as carrying, in their own natures, no reference to creation. The process has been lost.

The final outcome has been that philosophy and theology have been saddled with the problem of deriving the historic world of change from a changeless world of ultimate reality. Our whole conception of knowledge has been vitiated. The final wisdom has been pictured as the changeless contemplation of changeless reality. Knowledge in abstraction from action has been exalted. Action is thereby conceived as being concerned with a world of shadows. Plato's lecture on the "Good," with its emphasis on mathematics as then understood, is symbolic of this attitude which has haunted philosophy.

In those days, mathematics was the science of a static universe. Any transition was conceived as a transition of static forms. Today we conceive of forms of transition. The modern concept of an infinite series is the concept of a form of transition, namely, the character of the series as a whole is such a form. The notion of the sum of such a series is the notion of a final issue indicated by this form of transition.

The distorted attitude of attention to static forms has haunted philosophy, but it has not exclusively dominated it. The outstanding figures in the philosophic tradition have not achieved eminence solely by their championship of systems peculiar to themselves. Systematic thought has clarified insights, and has directed attention to aspects of experience which exemplify special systems. But the universe stretches beyond our finite powers of understanding. The great thinkers from whom we derive inspiration enjoyed insights beyond their own systems. They made statements hard to reconcile with the neat little ways of thought which we pin on to their names. For example, the same philosopher who emphasized the changeless mathematical entities as characteristic components of supreme reality, also elsewhere declared "life and motion" to belong to the essential character of reality. He thus asked "How do things function?" as a way of understanding how those things exist. Again, another philosopher who reduces the connection between the data of experience to mere succession of sense data, also appeals to the fact of "expectation." This derivation of expectation from succession is an intelligible fact to Hume, although his own system provides no elucidation of it. We do not experience mere succession. We discern forms of succession; and the presupposition of such forms haunts philosophic thought and dominates our daily experience.

Plato and Hume illustrate that system is essential for rational thought. But they also illustrate that the closed system is the death of living understanding. In their explanations they wander beyond all system. They thus illustrate in their own procedures that our primary insight is a mixture of clarity and vagueness. The finite focus of clarity fades into an environment of vagueness stretching into the darkness of what is merely beyond. The partly comprehended forms of succession dimly illuminate this environment within experience.

9. We require to understand how the mere existence of unchanging form requires its own immersion in the creation of a changing historic world. There is a form of creation. We require to understand how the unity of the universe requires its multiplicity. We require to understand how infinitude requires the finite.

We require to understand how each immediately present existence requires its past, antecedent to itself; and requires its future, an essential factor in its own existence. There are thus three factors within immediate existence—namely, past, present, and future. In this way immediacy of finite existence refuses to be deprived of that infinitude of extension which is its perspective.

Again we require to understand how mere matter-of-fact refuses to be deprived of its relevance to potentialities beyond its own actuality of realization. The very character of concrete realization—that is to say, of historic fact—is suffused with the potentialities which it excludes with varying types of relevance. In the present fact there are the various characteristics of the past, partly reproduced and partly excluded; there are the characteristics of concurrent facts in the present, partly shared in and partly excluded; there are the possibilities for the future, partly prepared for and partly excluded. The discussion of present fact apart from reference to past, to concurrent present, and to future, and from reference to the preservation or destruction of forms of creation is to rob the universe of essential importance. In the absence of perspective there is triviality.

For example, in some concert hall there is the immediate volume of sound in the immediate specious present. There is the symphonic form which is dominating the successive moments of experience. There is the sense of creative genius from which this realized example of symphonic form is derived. There is the sense of multiplicity of creative genius—the artists in the orchestra, the conductor, the composer. There is the sense of the variety of static forms immediately realized: the forms of instruments, the spatial distribution of the orchestra, the mathematical analysis of each momentary sound, the musical score. In the end we are left with four main modes of characterizing experience. There are, in the first place, three main aspects within aesthetic experience: the sense of genius, the sense of disclosure, the sense of frustration. We also retain three aspects of matter-of-fact: namely, the experiences of unity, of multitude, of transition.

We discern three primary grounds of division, namely, clarity and vagueness, order and disorder, the good and the bad.

Finally, there are two ultimate types of existence implicated in the creative process, the eternal forms with their dual existence in potential appetition and in realized fact, and realized fact with its dual ways of existence as the past in the present and as the immediacy of the present. Also the immediacy of the present harbours an appetition towards the unrealized future. How the thinker deals with these four modes of experience determines the shape of philosophy, and the influence of thought upon the practice of life.

Forms of Process

The topic of this, and of the next, lecture originates in the consideration of the various modes of unity exhibited by compositions within the historic world. Examples of such organizations are throbs of pulsation, molecules, stones, lives of plants, lives of animals, lives of men. The discussion then passes into the vaguer forms of unity, such as sociology in its widest meaning, laws of nature, spatio-temporal connections.

The argument passes to the consideration of that final mode of unity in virtue of which there exists stability of aim amid the multiple forms of potentiality, and in virtue of which there exists importance beyond the finite importance for the finite actuality. In other words, How does importance for the finite require importance for the infinite?

In this connection, Descartes discusses perfection. He chose a notion which is too limited and too ambiguous. He slipped into his discussion a false premise, namely, that one final perfection with static existence constitutes a notion which is relevant to our experience. He should have taken the wider notion of importance. In what sense is there "importance for the universe"? Does not "importance for the finite" involve the notion of "importance for the infinite"?

2. The first point to make is the transition from accident towards necessity as we pass from the smaller to the larger units of composition. There is a large element of accident in a single sentence of a lecture. The lecture as a whole reflects with some necessity the character of the lecturer as he composes it. The character of the lecturer arises from the moulding it receives from the social circumstances of his whole life. These social circumstances depend on the historic epoch, and this epoch is derivative from the evolution of life on this planet. Life on this planet depends on the order observed throughout the spatio-temporal stellar system, as disclosed in our experience. These special forms of order exhibit no final necessity whatsover. The laws of nature are forms of activity which happen to prevail within the vast epoch of activity which we dimly discern. A problem now arises. There are forms of order with vast extension throughout time. There is no necessity in their nature. But there is necessity that the importance of experience requires adequate stability of order. Complete confusion can be equated with complete frustration. And yet the transitions of history exhibit transitions of forms of order. Epoch gives way to epoch. If we insist on construing the new epoch in terms of the forms of order in its predecessor we see mere confusion. Also there is no sharp division. There are always forms of order partially dominant, and partially frustrated. Order is never complete; frustration is never complete. There is transition within the dominant order; and there is transition to new forms of dominant order. Such transition is a frustration of the prevalent dominance. And yet it is the realization of that vibrant novelty which elicits the excitement of life.

The essence of life is to be found in the frustrations of established order. The Universe refuses the deadening influence of complete conformity. And yet in its refusal, it passes towards novel order as a primary requisite for important experience. We have to explain the aim at forms of order, and the aim at novelty of order, and the measure of success, and the measure of failure. Apart from some understanding, however dim, of these characteristics of the historic process, we enjoy no rationality of experience.

The development of western philosophy has been hampered by the tacit presupposition of the necessity of static spatio-temporal, and physical forms of order. The development of scientific knowledge in the last two hundred years has completely swept away any ground for the assumption of such necessity. But the presupposition remains even among men of science. It is a tacit presupposition, among those who explicitly deny it. In current literature we find the same authors denying infractions of natural order, and denying any reason for such denial, and denying any justification for a philosophical search for reasons justifying their own denials.

What we have to explain is the trend towards order which is the overwhelming deliverance of experience. What we have also to explain is the frustration of order, and the absence of necessity in any particular form of order.

3. We must first examine the notion of "Process." The comprehension of this notion requires an analysis of the interweaving of data, form, transition, and issue. There is a rhythm of process whereby creation produces natural pulsation, each pulsation forming a natural unit of historic fact. In this way, amid the infinitude of the connected universe, we can discern vaguely finite units of fact. If process be fundamental to actuality, then each ultimate individual fact must be describable as process. The Newtonian description of matter abstracts matter from time. It conceives matter "at an instant." So does Descartes'

description. If process be fundamental such abstraction is erroneous.

We have now to consider in more detail this interweaving of data, form, transition, and issue which characterizes each unit of fact. We must however proceed by violent abstraction. Each fully realized fact has an infinitude of relations in the historic world and in the realm of form; namely, its perspective of the universe. We can only conceive it with respect to a minute selection of these relations. These relations, thus abstracted, require for their full understanding the infinitude from which we abstract. We experience more than we can analyse. For we experience the universe, and we analyse in our consciousness a minute selection of its details.

The data for any one pulsation of actuality consist of the full content of the antecedent universe as it exists in relevance to that pulsation. They are this universe conceived in its multiplicity of details. These multiplicities are antecedent pulsations, and also there are the variety of forms harboured in the nature of things, either as realized form or as potentialities for realization. Thus the data consist in what has been, what might have been, and what may be. And in these phrases the verb *to be* means some mode of relevance to historic actualities.

Such are the data; and from these data there emerges a process with a form of transition. This unit of process is the "specious present" of the actuality in question. It is a process of composition, of gradation, and of elimination. Every detail in the process of being actual involves its own gradation in reference to the other details. The effectiveness of any one such factor involves the elimination of elements in the data not to be reconciled with that detail playing that part in the process. Now elimination is a positive fact, so that the background of discarded data adds a tone of feeling to the whole pulsation. No fact of history, personal or social, is understood until we know what it has escaped and the narrowness of the escape. You cannot fully understand the history of the European races in North America, without reference to the double failure of Spanish domination over California in the nineteenth century, and over England in the sixteenth century.

All actuality involves the realization of form derived from factual data. It is both a composition of qualities, and it is also a form of composition. The form of composition dictates how those forms as thus realized in the data enter into a finite process of composition, thus achieving new actuality with its own exemplifications and discards. There is a form of process dealing with a complex form of data and issuing into a novel completion of actuality. But no actuality is a static fact. The historic character of the universe belongs to its essence. The completed fact is only to be understood as taking its place among the active data forming the future.

When we consider the process under examination as completed, we are already analysing an active datum for other creations. The universe is not a museum with its specimens in glass cases. Nor is the universe a perfectly drilled regiment with its ranks in step, marching forward with undisturbed poise. Such notions belong to the fable of modern science—a very useful fable when understood for what it is. Science deals with large average effects, important within certain modes of observation. But in the history of human thought no scientific conclusion has ever survived unmodified by radical increase in our subtleties of relevant knowledge.

4. In order to examine the notion of a form of transition, we will dwell on its simplest example. Consider arithmetic as being concerned with special forms of process. We shall here be contradicting the fashionable notion of "tautology." Conceive the fusion of two groups, each char-

acterized by triplicity, into a single group. The whole essence of the notion of "twice-three" is process, and "twice-three" expresses its special form of process. This form derives its peculiar character from two sources. One source is the triplicity of each of the two groups in process of fusion. This triplicity arises from some principle of individuation dominating the process of aggregation of each group. As a result of this principle, each group exemplifies three-ness. There is then a process of fusion of both groups into one. We are considering the characterization of this resultant group in terms of number. It is not true that this process of fusion necessarily issues in a group of six, in which the same principle of identifying individual things is preserved.

For example, consider drops of water, each drop with its own skin of surface tension. Let there be two groups, each of three drops. The process of fusion may result in coalescence so that one drop results; or it may result in shattering the original drops, so that a group of fifty drops appears. The process, normally presupposed in the phrase "twice-three," is such that the relevant principle of individuation is kept undisturbed. In such a case, twice-three is six. But this phrase "principle of individuation" has a vague interpretation. A doctor orders a dose of two teaspoonfuls. The dose is in fact taken in one dessert spoon. Thus the actual individualization into teaspoons may be unimportant, and may never be achieved.

The statement "twice-three is six" is referent to an unspecified principle of sustenance of character which is supposed to be maintained during the process of fusion. The phrase "twice-three" refers to a form of process of fusion sustaining this principle of individuation. Putting this in a more general statement, arithmetical phrases refer to special forms of process, issuing in a group characterized by some definite arithmetical character. The process has its strict form, and in the circumstances mentioned it issues in a complex entity with that character.

I am sorry to insist on this triviality at such wearisome length. Perhaps some of you will have recognized that I am contradicting a widespread belief. A prevalent modern doctrine is that the phrase "twice-three is six" is a tautology. This means that "twice-three" says the same thing as "six"; so that no new truth is arrived at in the sentence. My contention is that the sentence considers a process and its issue. Of course, the issue of one process is part of the material for processes beyond itself. But in respect to the abstraction "twice-three is six," the phrase "twice-three" indicates a form of fluent process and "six" indicates a characterization of the completed fact.

We are naïve in our interpretation of language and of symbolism. We neglect subtle differences of meaning. If we say that "six is not equal to seven," we are denying the identity of "six" and "seven." In this phrase, the word *equality* means identity. If we say that "twice-three is six," we are saying that the issue of a process is an entity with the character "six." If we are saying that "twice-three is equal to the sum of two and four," we are saying that two distinct processes issue in compositions with the same numerical character. The meanings of *equality*—or of the word *is*—differ in each of these cases. My final point is that mathematics is concerned with certain forms of process issuing into forms which are components for further process. In the previous lecture, we noted that the concept of a form of process gave its meaning to the concept of an infinite series, as employed in mathematics.

This discussion is a belated reminder to Plato that his eternal mathematical forms are essentially referent to process. This is his own doctrine when he refers to the necessity of life and motion. But only intermittently did he keep it in mind. He was apt to identify process with mere appearance, and to conceive of absolute reality as devoid of transition. For him, in this mood, mathematics belonged to changeless eternity. He then has accepted tautology.

5. The nature of any type of existence can only be explained by reference to its implication in creative activity, essentially involving three factors: namely, data, process with its form relevant to these data, and issue into datum for further process—data, process, issue.

The alternative is the reduction of the universe to a barren tautological absolute, with a dream of life and motion. The discovery of mathematics, like all discoveries, both advanced human understanding, and also produced novel modes of error. Its error was the introduction of the doctrine of form, devoid of life and motion.

The "supreme being" of Greek philosophy was conceived by thinkers under the influence of the then recent development of mathematics, when the active-minded Greeks came into contact with Egyptian thought. They misconceived the relevance of mathematical notions. All mathematical notions have reference to process of intermingling. The very notion of number refers to the process from the individual units to the compound group. The final number belongs to no one of the units; it characterizes the way in which the group unity has been attained. Thus even the statement "six equals six" need not be construed as a mere tautology. It can be taken to mean that six as dominating a special form of combination issues in six as a character of a datum for further process. There is no such entity as a mere static number. There are only numbers playing their parts in various processes conceived in abstraction from the world-process.

The notion of the world-process is therefore to be conceived as the notion of the totality of process. The notion of a supreme being must apply to an actuality in process of composition, an actuality not confined to the data of any special epoch in the historic field. Its actuality is founded on the infinitude of its conceptual appetition, and its form of process is derived from the fusion of this appetition with the data received from the world-process. Its function in the world is to sustain the aim at vivid experience. It is the reservoir of potentiality and the coördination of achievement. The form of its process is relevant to the data from which the process is initiated. The issue is the unified composition which assumes its function as a datum operative in the future historic world.

The data of our experience are of two kinds. They can be analysed into realized matter-of-fact and into potentialities for matter-of-fact. Further, these potentialities can be analysed into pure abstract potentialities apart from special relevance to realization in the data or the issue, and into potentialities entertained by reason of some closeness of relevance to such realization. These potentialities entertained in respect to their close relevance are the agents dictating the form of composition which produces the issue. This dictation of a form of composition involves the birth of an energetic determination whereby the data are subject to preservation and discard.

In so far as there is large mutual conformity in the data, the energetic form of composition is such as to transmit this conformity to the issue, thereby preserving that uniformity for the future. We have here the basis of the large-scale preservation of identities, amid minor changes. The planets, the stones, the living things all witness to the wide preservation of identity. But equally they witness to the partiality of such preservation. Nothing in realized matter-of-fact retains complete identity with its antecedent self. This self-identity in the sphere of realized fact is only partial. It holds for certain purposes. It dominates certain kinds of process. But in other sorts of process, the differences are important, and the self-identity is an interesting fable. For the purpose of inheriting real estate, the identity of the man of thirty years of age with the former baby of ten months is dominant. For the purpose of navigating a yacht, the differences between the man and the child are essential; the identity then sinks into a metaphysical irrelevancy. In so far as identities are preserved, there are orderly laws of nature. In so far as identities decay, these laws are subject to modification. But the modification itself may be lawful. The change in the individual may exhibit a law of change, as, for example, the change from baby to fully-grown animal. And yet such laws of change are themselves liable to change. For example, species flourish and decay; civilizations rise and fall; heavenly bodies gradually form, and pass through sequences of stages.

In any of these examples, as the changes occur, new types of existence are rendered possible, subject to new laws of nature dependent upon that new environment. In other words, the data, the forms of process, and the issues into new data, are all dependent upon their epoch and upon the forms of process dominant in that epoch.

Nothing is more interesting to watch than the emotional disturbance produced by any unusual disturbance of the forms of process. The slow drift is accepted. But when for human experience quick changes arrive, human nature passes into hysteria. For example, gales, thunderstorms, earthquakes, revolutions in social habits, violent illnesses, destructive fires, battles, are all occasions of special excitement. There are perfectly good reasons for this energetic reaction to quick change. My point is the exhibition of our emotional reactions to the dominance of lawful order, and to the breakdown of such order. When fundamental change arrives, sometimes heaven dawns, sometimes hell yawns open.

6. Too much attention has been directed to the mere datum and the mere issue. The essence of existence lies in the transition from datum to issue. This is the process of self-determination. We must not conceive of a dead datum with passive form. The datum is impressing itself upon this process, conditioning its forms. We must not dwell mainly on the issue. The immediacy of existence is then past and over. The vividness of life lies in the transition, with its forms aiming at the issue. Actuality in its essence is aim at self-formation.

One main doctrine, developed in these lectures, is that "existence" (in any of its senses) cannot be abstracted from "process." The notions of process and existence presuppose each other. One deduction from this thesis is that the notion of a point in process is fallacious. The concept of point is here meant to imply that process can be analysed into compositions of final realities, themselves devoid of process.

For example, consider the notion of a moment of time devoid of any temporal spread—for example, at noon on such and such a day. Such a notion is the concept of a point devoid of process. Again, a point in space is another such example. On the contrary, the extension of space is the ghost of transition. It is only to be experienced by some process of transition. This truth has, within the last thirty years, conquered modern physics in the somewhat naïve form of doctrines about light.

The general principle, underlying these special cases, is that the erroneous notions of process devoid of individualities, and of individualities devoid of process, can never be adjusted to each other. If you start with either of these falsehoods, you must dismiss the other as meaningless.

The notion of number, as elaborated in arithmetic, has been traditionally treated with this bias towards such an erroneous separation. Each individual thing is devoid of numerosity; whereas, a static group is characterized by number. In this way process seems to be absent in our treatment of arithmetic. Thus mathematics has been conceived as the test case, which is the citadel for a false metaphysics.

When Plato thought of mathematics he conceived of a changeless world of form, and contrasted it with the mere imitation in the world of transition. Yet when Plato thought of the realities of action, he swayed to the opposite point of view. He called for life and motion to rescue forms from a meaningless void.

In these lectures Plato's second doctrine, of life and motion, has been adopted. The mathematical modes of fusion, such as "addition," "multiplication," "serial form," and so on, have been construed as forms of process. The very notion of "multiplicity" itself has been construed as abstraction from the form of process whereby data acquire a unity of issue into a novel datum.

7. Process and individuality require each other. In separation all meaning evaporates. The form of process (or, in other words, the appetition) derives its character from the individuals involved, and the characters of the individuals can only be understood in terms of the process in which they are implicated.

A difficult problem arises from this doctrine. How can the notion of any generality of reasoning be justified? For if the process depends on the individuals, then with different individuals the form of process differs. Accordingly, what has been said of one process cannot be said of another process. The same difficulty applies to the notion of the identity of an individual conceived as involved in different processes. Our doctrine seems to have destroyed the very basis of rationality.

The point is that every individual thing infects any process in which it is involved, and thus any process cannot be considered in abstraction from particular things involved. Also the converse holds. Hence the absolute generality of logic and of mathematics vanish. Also induction loses any security. For in other circumstances, there will be other results.

In approaching this problem, the first point to notice is that its difficulty is in accordance with common sense. The distinctions between various sciences, and various topics for study, illustrate this point. No one would study geology as a preparation for appreciation of the sonnets of Shakespeare or the fugues of Bach. The things discussed in geology are so different from sonnets and so different from fugues. The result is that the interconnections discussed in a treatise on geology are very different from those disclosed in the structure of a sonnet or of a fugue. But faint analogies do occur. Sometimes these analogies rise in importance. For example, the Greeks discovered analogies between the lengths of strings and the harmonies of musical notes, and between the measurements of the dimensions of a building and the beauty of the structure.

Thus the differences arising from diversities are not absolute. Analogies survive amid diversity. The procedure of rationalism is the discussion of analogy. The limitation of rationalism is the inescapable diversity. The development of civilized thought can be described as the discovery of identities amid diversity. For example, the discovery of identities of number as between a group of days and a group of fishes.

The whole understanding of the world consists in the analysis of process in terms of the identities and diversities of the individuals involved. The peculiarities of the individuals are reflected in the peculiarities of the common process which is their interconnection. We can start our investigation from either end; namely, we can understand the process and thence consider the characterization of the individuals; or we can characterize the individuals and conceive them as formative of the relevant process. In truth, the distinction is only one of emphasis.

But this possibility of abstraction, whereby individuals and the forms of process constituting their existence can be considered separately, brings out a fundamental intuition which lies at the basis of all thought. This intuition consists in the essential passage from experience of individual fact to the conception of character. Thence we proceed to the concept of the stability of character amidst the succession of facts. Thence we proceed to the concept of the partial identity of successive facts in a given route of succession. Thence we proceed to the potentiality of the facts for maintaining such partial identity amid such succession.

In other words, as soon as we abstract, so as to separate the notions of serial forms and of individual facts involved, we necessarily introduce the notion of potentiality: namely, the potentiality of the facts for the series and of the series for the facts. All our knowledge consists in conceiving possible adjustments of series and of individual facts to each other. We say in effect, such and such facts are consistent with such and such serial forms. We are considering possibilities for individuals and possibilities for series. The mere immediate exemplification is only one aspect of our experience.

8. The notion of potentiality is fundamental for the understanding of existence, as soon as the notion of process is admitted. If the universe be interpreted in terms of static actuality, then potentiality vanishes. Everything is just what it is. Succession is mere appearance, rising from the limitation of perception. But if we start with process as fundamental, then the actualities of the present are deriving their characters from the process, and are bestowing their characters upon the future. Immediacy is the realization of the potentialities of the past, and is the storehouse

of the potentialities of the future. Hope and fear, joy and disillusion, obtain their meaning from the potentialities essential in the nature of things. We are following a trail in hope, or are fleeing from the pursuit in fear. The potentialities in immediate fact constitute the driving force of process.

At this point the discussion must be halted. It has run into exaggeration. The essence of the universe is more than process. The alternative metaphysical doctrine, of reality devoid of process, would never have held the belief of great men, unless it expressed some fundamental aspect of our experience. For example, Newton's belief in absolute space may be mistaken. All the same it bears witness to the fact of the obviousness to him of factors in the universe to which the notion of process does not apply. At least the potentiality of spatial relations among the realizations of history stood for him as a timeless fact. He did not state it in this way. This formulation tones down his own belief in the independent actuality of space.

But as expressed in this way, the notion of spatial relations is an example of connected forms with overwhelming relevance to the present epoch of history. Also it illustrates the main principle on which induction is based. This principle is that form of process chiefly derives from the dominant facts involved and thence tends to sustain itself so as to govern realizations in its own future. This is the doctrine of the varying relevance of potential forms. Thus the doctrine of the potentiality of the present to characterize the realizations of the future lies hidden in the beliefs of Bacon and of Newton. It is the sense of the form having a dual activity in the present. It characterizes the present and it thereby fashions the form of process in the future.

Two other names must be added. Plato with his supreme realm of forms, and Leibniz with his monads each with its form of process. Leibniz's doctrine is curiously reminiscent of Descartes' science of analytical geometry with its curves, each expressed by an algebraic equation, which is the form for the description of the curve. The difficulty is to relate the static form to the active process. There is an analogous difficulty in relating the static immediacy of fact to the historic process with its past and its future. There is the further problem to express the interconnections of facts, each with its measure of self-sufficiency. Each fact is just that limited thing that it is. How then do facts require each other? Finally, each immediate fact is a realization of itself. In what sense, then, can a fact harbour potentiality, which is the capacity of form for realization? In other words, how can the realization of form involve in its own nature reference to the realization of other forms in other occasions?

The topics thus enumerated are generalized statements of the commonplaces of experience. They merely express what of course our lives mean to us in every moment of experience. For this very reason language fails in its analysis. We do not have to indicate for each other the necessities of existence. Language mainly presupposes the necessities and emphasizes the accidents. We rarely mention what must be present. We do mention what might be absent. The whole difficulty of philosophic discussion is this feebleness of language. The title of one outstanding philosophic treatise in the English language, belonging to the generation now passing, is "Space, Time, and Deity." By this phrase, Samuel Alexander places before us the problem which haunts the serious thought of mankind. "Time" refers to the transitions of process, "space" refers to the static necessity of each form of interwoven existence, and "deity" expresses the lure of the ideal which is the potentiality beyond immediate fact.

9. Apart from time there is no meaning for purpose, hope, fear, energy. If there be no historic process, then

everything is what it is, namely, a mere fact. Life and motion are lost. Apart from space, there is no consummation. Space expresses the halt for attainment. It symbolizes the complexity of immediate realization. It is the fact of accomplishment. Time and space express the universe as including the essence of transition and the success of achievement. The transition is real, and the achievement is real. The difficulty is for language to express one of them without explaining away the other.

Finally, there is deity, which is that factor in the universe whereby there is importance, value, and ideal beyond the actual. It is by reference of the spatial immediacies to the ideals of deity that the sense of worth beyond ourselves arises. The unity of a transcendent universe, and the multiplicity of realized actualities, both enter into our experience by this sense of deity. Apart from this sense of transcendent worth, the otherness of reality would not enter into our consciousness. There must be value beyond ourselves. Otherwise every thing experienced would be merely a barren detail in our own solipsist mode of existence. We owe to the sense of deity the obviousness of the many actualities of the world, and the obviousness of the unity of the world for the preservation of the values realized and for the transition to ideals beyond realized fact.

Thus, space, time, and deity are general terms which indicate three types of reflective notions. The understanding of the nature of things in terms of such concepts is what distinguishes the human species from the other animals. The distinction is not absolute. The higher animals show every sign of understandings and of devotions which pass beyond the immediate enjoyments of immediate fact. Also the life of each human being is mainly a dumb passage from immediacy to immediacy devoid of the illumination of higher reflection. But when all analogies between animal life and human nature have been stressed, there remains the vast gap in respect to the influence of reflective experience. This reflective experience exhibits three main characteristics which require each other for their full understanding. There are the experiences of joint association, which are the spatial experiences. There are the experiences of origination from a past and of determination towards a future. These are temporal experiences.

There are experiences of ideals—of ideals entertained, of ideals aimed at, of ideals achieved, of ideals defaced. This is the experience of the deity of the universe. The intertwining of success and failure in respect to this final experience is essential. We thereby experience a relationship to a universe other than ourselves. We are essentially measuring ourselves in respect to what we are not. A solipsist experience cannot succeed or fail, for it would be all that exists. There would be no standard of comparison. Human experience explicitly relates itself to an external standard. The universe is thus understood as including a source of ideals.

The effective aspect of this source is deity as immanent in the present experience. The sense of historic importance is the intuition of the universe as everlasting process, unfading in its deistic unity of ideals.

Thus there is an essential relevance between deity and historic process. For this reason, the form of process is not wholly dependent upon derivation from the past. As epochs decay amid futility and frustration, the form of process derives other ideals involving novel forms of order.

Science investigates the past, and predicts the future in terms of the forms of past achievement. But as the present becomes self-destructive of its inherited modes of importance, then the deistic influence implants in the historic process new aims at other ideals.

Science is concerned with the facts of bygone transition. History relates the aim at ideals. And between science and history, lies the operation of the deistic impulse of energy. It is the religious impulse in the world which transforms the dead facts of science into the living drama of history. For this reason science can never foretell the perpetual novelty of history.

Civilized Universe

In this lecture we seek the evidence for that conception of the universe which is the justification for the ideals characterizing the civilized phases of human society.

We have been assuming as self-evident the many actualities, their forms of coördination in the historic process, their separate importance, and their joint importance for the universe in its unity. It must be clearly understood, as stated in the earlier lectures, that we are not arguing from well-defined premises. Philosophy is the search for premises. It is not deduction. Such deductions as occur are for the purpose of testing the starting points by the evidence of the conclusions.

A special science takes the philosophic assumptions and transforms them into comparative clarity by narrowing them to the forms of the special topic in question. Also even in reasoning thus limited to special topics, there is no absolute conclusiveness in the deductive logic. The premises have assumed their limited clarity by reason of presuming the irrelevance of considerations extraneous to the assigned topic. The premises are conceived in the simplicity of their individual isolation. But there can be no logical test for the possibility that deductive procedure, leading to the elaboration of compositions, may introduce into relevance considerations from which the primitive notions of the topic have been abstracted. The mutual conformity of the various perspectives can never be adequately determined.

The history of science is full of such examples of sciences bursting through the bounds of their original assumptions. Even in pure abstract logic as applied to arithmetic, it has within the last half century been found necessary to introduce a doctrine of types in order to correct the omissions of the original premises.

Thus deductive logic has not the coercive supremacy which is conventionally conceded to it. When applied to concrete instances, it is a tentative procedure, finally to be judged by the self-evidence of its issues. This doctrine places philosophy on a pragmatic basis. But the meaning of "pragmatism" must be given its widest extension. In much modern thought, it has been limited by arbitrary specialist assumptions. There should be no pragmatic exclusion of self-evidence by dogmatic denial. Pragmatism is simply an appeal to that self-evidence which sustains itself in civilized experience. Thus pragmatism ultimately appeals to the wide self-evidence of civilization, and to the self-evidence of what we mean by "civilization."

Before we finally dismiss deductive logic, it is well to note the function of the "variable" in logical reason. In this connection the term *variable* is applied to a symbol, occurring in a propositional form which merely indicates any entity to which the propositional form can be validly applied, so as to constitute a determinate proposition. Also the variable, though undetermined, sustains its identity throughout the arguments. The notion originally assumed importance in algebra, in the familiar letters such as x, y, z indicating any numbers. It also appears somewhat tentatively in the Aristotelian syllogisms, where names such as "Socrates," indicate "any man, the same throughout the argument."

The use of the variable is to indicate the self-identity of some use of "any" throughout a train of reasoning. For example in elementary algebra when x first appears it means "any number." But in that train of reasoning, the reappearance of x always means "the same number" as in that original appearance. Thus the variable is an ingenious combination of the vagueness of any with the definiteness of a particular indication.

In logical reasoning, which proceeds by the use of the variable, there are always two tacit presuppositions—one is that the definite symbols of composition can retain the same meaning as the reasoning elaborates novel compositions. The other presupposition is that this self-identity of each variable can be preserved when the variable is replaced by some definite instance. Complete self-identity can never be preserved in any advance to novelty. The only question is, as to whether the loss is relevant to the purposes of the argument. The baby in the cradle, and the grown man in middle age, are in some senses identical and in other senses diverse. Is the train of argument in its conclusions substantiated by the identity or vitiated by the diversity?

We thus dismiss deductive logic as a major instrument for metaphysical discussion. Such discussion is concerned with the eliciting of self-evidence. Apart from such self-evidence, deduction fails. Thus logic presupposes metaphysics.

2. What is the dominating insight whereby we presuppose ourselves as actualities within a world of actualities? There can be no argument from a purely subjective experience of qualitative details so as validly to infer a world of actualities coördinate with ourselves. A "form of

reception" will then be simply a mode of make-belief. In other words, a form of reception is reduced to an account of our solipsist existence. It describes our individual experience of a display of qualitative pattern. It gives an account of an activity within us. It gives no account of ourselves as activities among other activities. It misses the point that we know ourselves as creatures in a world of creatures. We are reduced to an enjoyment of mere appearance. With such assumptions there are no data for the insight into a world of many coördinated actualities.

In the discussion of our experience, the first point for notice is the superficial variability in our clear consciousness of qualitative detail. The decisive consciousness that *this* is red, and *that* is loud, and *this other* is square, results from an effort of concentration and elimination. Also it is never sustained. There is always a flickering variation, varied by large scale transference of attention. Consciousness is an ever-shifting process of abstracting shifting quality from a massive process of essential existence. It emphasizes. And yet, if we forget the background, the result is triviality.

Concentration of attention on sheer qualitative detail can result in consciousness of mere succession of such detail. For example, we record a red-and-green pattern succeeded by a blue-and-grey pattern, the experience being closed by a clear bell-like sound. There is a qualitative subjective experience. That and nothing more. The whole meaningless. This is the result of obtaining a clear-cut experience by concentrating on the abstractions of consciousness.

But we are conscious of more than clarity. The importance of clarity does not arise until we have interpreted it in terms of the vast issues vaguely haunting the fullness of existence.

It is here that the prominent epistemology of the modern centuries has been so weak. It has interpreted the totality of experience as a mere reaction to an initial clarity of sensa. The result is that the reaction is limited to the data provided by the sensa. Such modern schools of philosophic thought can simply ask, What is the sensible emotional reaction to a red-and-green pattern, succeeded by a blue-and-grey pattern, succeeded by a clear bell-like sound? The answer is, what you like, except you are a highbrow intellectual when you will follow the current reactions of Greenwich Village and Harvard, if you are American, and of Bloomsbury and Oxford, if you are English.

In other words, the mass of our moral, emotional, and purposive experience is rendered trivial and accidental. The whole notion of our massive experience conceived as a reaction to clearly envisaged details is fallacious. The relationship should be inverted. The details are a reaction to the totality. They add definition. They introduce powers of judgment. They exalt men above animals, and animals above vegetables, and vegetables beyond stones, always provided that they are kept in their proper relation to the soil from which they originate. They are interpretive and not originative. What is original is the vague totality.

Of course, the clarity of experience does originate further experience, by reason of its very clarity. But this origination is a secondary fact, and is not the basis of the whole. We enter the room already equipped with an active aesthetic experience, and we are charmed with the forms and colouring of the furniture. The sensory experience of the room adds vividness and point to an activity of feeling already possessed.

3. At the base of our existence is the sense of "worth." Now worth essentially presupposes that which is worthy. Here the notion of worth is not to be construed in a purely eulogistic sense. It is the sense of existence for its own sake, of existence which is its own justification, of existence with its own character.

The discrimination of detail is definitely a secondary process, which may or may not assume importance. There is the germ of discrimination, which may or may not flower into a varied experience. The dim decision is a large-scale judgment—namely, avoidance or maintenance. The stage of analysis into details, of which some are to be discarded, others are to be maintained, has not arrived. There is simply the large-scale feeling as to the totality—avoid it or maintain it.

Again the primitive stage of discrimination is not primarily qualitative. It is the vague grasp of reality, dissecting it into a threefold scheme, namely, "The Whole," "That Other," and "This-My-Self."

This is primarily a dim division. The sense of totality obscures the analysis into self and others. Also this division is primarily based on the sense of existence as a value experience. Namely, the total value experience is discriminated into this value experience and those value experiences. There is the vague sense of many which are one; and of one which includes the many. Also there are two senses of the one—namely, the sense of the one which is all, and the sense of the one among the many.

The fundamental *basis* of this description is that our experience is a value experience, expressing a vague sense of maintenance or discard; and that this value experience differentiates itself in the sense of many existences with value experience; and that this sense of the multiplicity of value experiences again differentiates it into the totality of value experience, and the many other value experiences, and the egoistic value experience. There is the feeling of the ego, the others, the totality. This is the vague, basic presentation of the differentiation of existence, in its enjoyment of discard and maintenance. We are, each of us, one among others; and all of us are embraced in the unity of the whole.

The basis of democracy is the common fact of value experience, as constituting the essential nature of each pulsation of actuality. Everything has some value for itself, for others, and for the whole. This characterizes the meaning of actuality. By reason of this character, constituting reality, the conception of morals arises. We have no right to deface the value experience which is the very essence of the universe. Existence, in its own nature, is the upholding of value intensity. Also no unit can separate itself from the others, and from the whole. And yet each unit exists in its own right. It upholds value intensity for itself, and this involves sharing value intensity with the universe. Everything that in any sense exists has two sides, namely, its individual self and its signification in the universe. Also either of these aspects is a factor in the other.

So far, we have been considering the dim foundation of experience. In animal experience there supervenes a process of keen discrimination of quality. The sense experiences, such as sight, sound, smell, taste, touch, and so on, are distinguished. Also within each such species of quality, clear distinctions are discerned, for example, red and green, distinctions of note, distinctions of taste.

With the rise of clear sensations relating themselves to the universe of value-feeling, the world of human experience is defined.

4. At this point, the preceding exposition must be reviewed. It is evident that the current doctrine of epistemology has been completely inverted. This current doctrine culminated in the eighteenth century with Hume's *Treatise*. It bases itself upon the well-defined factors in our experience. Undoubtedly there are these sensa, such as sensations of colour, sound, and so on. It is then assumed that because they are definite, therefore they are fundamental.

The other factors in experiences are therefore to be

construed as derivative, in the sense of owing their origin to these sensa. Emotions, aspirations, hopes, fears, love, and hate, intentions, and recollections are merely concerned with sensa. Apart from sensa, they would be non-existent.

This is the doctrine which in this lecture is being denied. The only mode of decision can be by an appeal to the self-evidence of experience. In Hume's *Treatise,* this appeal is the basis on which he founds his doctrine.

In opposition to Hume's interpretation of experience, the first point to notice is that these distinct sensa are the most variable elements in our lives. We can shut our eyes, or be permanently blind. None the less we are alive. We can be deaf. And yet we are alive. We can shift and transmute these details of experience almost at will.

Further, in the course of a day our experience varies with respect to its entertainment of sensa. We are wide-awake, we doze, we meditate, we sleep. There is nothing basic in the clarity of our entertainment of sensa. Also in the course of our lives, we start in the womb, in the cradle, and we gradually acquire the art of correlating our fundamental experience to the clarity of newly-acquired sensa.

Again, human beings are merely one species in the throng of existences. There are the animals, the vegetables, the microbes, the living cells, the inorganic physical activities. At the beginning of science, nature was surveyed as including diversities of species and genera, separated by impassable boundaries. Today the doctrine of evolution reigns. We need not necessarily conceive this doctrine as implying evolution upwards. What we do observe is the historic transition from species to species, and genera to genera. The qualitative experiences of the various animals seem to be vastly different. In some respects, more keenly felt than among human beings—for example, the sense of

smell by some dogs. In other respects, there is reason to
suspect a certain dimness of such experience in living
things with low types of bodily organization. And yet they
react to the external world.

In other words, reaction to the environment is not in
proportion to clarity of sensory experience. Any such
doctrine would sweep away the whole of modern physical
science as being expressed in terms of irrelevancies. Reaction does not depend upon sense experience for its initiation.

Now confine the argument to human experience, which
we know at first hand. This experience does not depend
for its excellence simply upon clarity of sense experience.
The specialist in clarity sinks to an animal level—the hound
for smell, the eagle for sight.

Human beings are amateurs in sense experience. The
direct, vivid clarity does not dominate so as to obscure the
infinite variety involved in the composition of reality. The
sense experience is an abstraction which illustrates and
stimulates the completeness of actuality. It increases importance. But the importance thus elicited is more than a
colour scheme of red, white, and blue. It involves the
infinitude of actuality, hidden in its finitude of realization.

5. Descartes, following a tradition stretching back to
the very origin of philosophy, derives a proof of the existence of God from the notion of perfection. His argument
fails, because he abstracts God from the historic universe.
Thus the conclusion depends upon meaningless phrases
respecting the unknown. We and our relationships are in
the universe.

The starting point of philosophy is the determination
of that aspect of experience which most fully exhibits the
universal necessities of existence. In answer to this problem Descartes gave the formula "clarity and distinctness."
He thereby inevitably prepared the way for Hume in the

next century. The immense value of the philosophic discussions produced by Descartes and by Hume, arises from the fact that neither of them consistently followed this formula. Undoubtedly the clear and distinct factors in human experience are the high-grade sensa. We have been considering the reasons for the conclusion that these distinct sensory factors are comparatively superficial elements in our lives.

Nothing is more astonishing in the history of philosophic thought than the naïve way in which our association with our human bodies is assumed. The unity of man and his body is taken for granted. Where does my body end and the external world begin? For example, my pen is external; my hand is part of my body; and my finger nails are part of my body. Also the breath as it passes in and out of my lungs from my mouth and throat fluctuates in its bodily relationship. Undoubtedly the body is very vaguely distinguishable from external nature. It is in fact merely one among other natural objects.

And yet, the unity "body and mind" is the obvious complex which constitutes the one human being. Our bodily experience is the basis of existence. How is it to be characterized? In the first place, it is not primarily an experience of sense data, in the clear and distinct sense of that term. The internal functioning of a healthy body provides singularly few sense data, primarily associated with itself. When such sense data appear, we send for a doctor. They are mostly aches and pains. And yet our feeling of bodily unity is a primary experience. It is an experience so habitual and so completely a matter of course that we rarely mention it. No one ever says, Here am I, and I have brought my body with me.

In what does this intimacy of relationship consist? The body is the basis of our emotional and purposive experience. It determines the way in which we react to the clear sensa. It determines the fact that we enjoy sensa. But the eye strain in sight is not the eye sight. We see with our eyes; we do not see our eyes.

The body is that portion of nature with which each moment of human experience intimately coöperates. There is an inflow and outflow of factors between the bodily actuality and the human experience, so that each shares in the existence of the other. The human body provides our closest experience of the interplay of actualities in nature.

Ordinary language, and the sciences of physiology and psychology, supply the evidence. This evidence is three fold: namely, the body is part of nature, the body supplies the basis of emotional and sensory activities, and the agitations of human experience pass into subsequent bodily functionings.

The body is that part of nature whose functionings are so coördinated as to be reciprocally coördinated with the functionings of the corresponding human experience. There is a transfer of types of agitation.

So long as nature was conceived in terms of the passive, instantaneous existence of bits of matter, according to Newton or Democritus, a difficulty arises. For there is an essential distinction between matter at an instant and the agitations of experience. But this conception of matter has now been swept away. Analogous notions of activity, and of forms of transition, apply to human experience and to the human body. Thus bodily activities and forms of experience can be construed in terms of each other. Also the body is part of nature. Thus we finally construe the world in terms of the type of activities disclosed in our intimate experience.

6. This conclusion must not be distorted. The fallacious notion of passive matter has by a reaction led to a distorted account of human experience. Human nature

has been described in terms of its vivid accidents, and not of its existential essence. The description of its essence must apply to the unborn child, to the baby in its cradle, to the state of sleep, and to that vast background of feeling hardly touched by consciousness. Clear, conscious discrimination is an accident of human existence. It makes us human. But it does not make us exist. It is of the essence of our humanity. But it is an accident of our existence.

What is our primary experience which lies below and gives its meaning to our conscious analysis of qualitative detail? In our analysis of detail we are presupposing a background which supplies a meaning. These vivid accidents accentuate something which is already there. We require to describe that factor in our experience which, being a matter of course, does not enter prominently into conversation. There is no need to mention it. For this reason language is very ineffective for the exposition of metaphysics.

Our enjoyment of actuality is a realization of worth, good or bad. It is a value experience. Its basic expression is—Have a care, here is something that matters! Yes—that is the best phrase—the primary glimmering of consciousness reveals, something that matters.

This experience provokes attention, dim and, all but, subconscious. Attention yields a three-fold character in the "Something that matters." "Totality," "Externality," and "Internality" are the primary characterizations of "that which matters." They are not to be conceived as clear, analytic concepts. Experience awakes with these dim presuppositions to guide its rising clarity of detailed analysis. They are presuppositions in the sense of expressing the sort of obviousness which experience exhibits. There is the totality of actual fact; there is the externality of many facts; there is the internality of this experiencing which lies within the totality.

These three divisions are on a level. No one in any sense precedes the other. There is the whole fact containing within itself my fact and the other facts. Also the dim meaning of fact—or actuality—is intrinsic importance for itself, for the others, and for the whole.

7. Of course all our terms of speech are too special, and refer too explicitly to higher stages of experience. For this reason, philosophy is analogous to imaginative art. It suggests meaning beyond its mere statements. On the whole, elaborate phrases enshrine the more primitive meanings.

Also as disclosure develops, facts disclose themselves as stages in the transitions of history. Importance reveals itself as transitions of emotion. My importance is my emotional worth now, embodying in itself derivations from the whole, and from the other facts, and embodying in itself reference to future creativity.

These embodiments both unify the many facts in the experiencing self, and at the same time differentiate these facts by their variety of reference to that self. Some facts have such closeness of reference to the immediate self that an intimate unity with them is claimed. In this way, the concept of self-identical enduring personal existence dawns. It is the concept of one person with many stages of existence. But the basis of all experience is this immediate stage of experiencing, which is myself now. Also the external facts, as disclosed in experiencing, tend more vaguely and flittingly to group themselves in the same way.

But the sense of importance is not exclusively referent to the experiencing self. It is exactly this vague sense which differentiates itself into the disclosure of the whole, the many, and the self. It is the importance of the others which melts into the importance of the self. Actuality is the self-enjoyment of importance. But this self-enjoyment has the character of the self-enjoyment of others melting into the enjoyment of the one self. The most explicit example of this is our realization of those other actualities, which we conceive as ourselves in our recent past, fusing their self-enjoyment with our immediate present. This is only the most vivid instance of the unity of the universe in each individual actuality.

The main point of this description is the concept of actuality as something that matters, by reason of its own self-enjoyment, which includes enjoyment of others and transitions towards the future.

Qualitative discrimination now arrives in the formation of the completed experience. The variety of quality is infinite. Thus every description is narrowed by some specialty of quality which is unconsciously presupposed.

There is the dim qualification enjoyed by the lowest types of actuality. There are the clear, distinct qualities enjoyed in human experience. There is every stage in between, and there are numberless stages which human experience has never touched. Undoubtedly, if we may trust our memories of the variety of human experience, the discrimination of quality immensely increases the intensity of experience. The sense of importance is a function of the analysis of experienced quality. It is hardly too much to say this. But it is too much; or rather, it is too simple an explanation. It does seem invariably the case, that the intrinsic importance of an experience requires a large clarity of analysis for one of its factors. Here the phrase "intrinsic importance" means "importance for itself."

But the whole point of this exposition is that our discrimination is exercised upon an experienced world. This world is the subject matter for qualitative discrimination. Civilization involves the understanding of the given world in respect to its qualifications.

8. This doctrine exactly inverts Hume's point of view, and the variant points of view derived from his doctrines.

Hume makes the qualifications primary; and the world is introduced as a secondary conjecture. It is to be noticed that our exposition is nothing else than the expansion of the insight that power is the basis of our notions of substance. This notion of power is to be found in Locke and in Plato, flittingly expressed and never developed. Our experience starts with a sense of power, and proceeds to the discrimination of individualities and their qualities.

Another consequence is that actuality is in its essence composition. Power is the compulsion of composition. Every other type of composition is a halfway stage in the attainment of actuality. The final actuality has the unity of power. The essence of power is the drive towards aesthetic worth for its own sake. All power is a derivative from this fact of composition attaining worth for itself. There is no other fact. Power and importance are aspects of this fact. It constitutes the drive of the universe. It is efficient cause, maintaining its power of survival. It is final cause, maintaining in the creature its appetition for creation.

The sense of externality is based on the primary self-analysis of the process of composition. This analysis discloses factors in the composition, with their own self-enjoyment and contributing that self-enjoyment to the immediate composition in which they are factors.

There are two types of such factors. In one type there are the many factors which form the historic environment for the new creation in the historic process. They are factors in the new composition which in its completion is one of themselves. This is a primary deliverance of experience, and if philosophical dictionaries have no single words to express it—so much the worse for the dictionaries.

9. The second type of factor has, by the nature of the case, only one example. It is that factor disclosed in our sense of the value, for its own sake, of the totality of historic fact in respect to its essential unity. There is a

unity in the universe, enjoying value and (by its immanence) sharing value. For example, take the subtle beauty
of a flower in some isolated glade of a primeval forest.
No animal has ever had the subtlety of experience to enjoy
its full beauty. And yet this beauty is a grand fact in the
universe. When we survey nature and think however
flitting and superficial has been the animal enjoyment of
its wonders, and when we realize how incapable the separate cells and pulsations of each flower are of enjoying the
total effect—then our sense of the value of the details for
the totality dawns upon our consciousness. This is the
intuition of holiness, the intuition of the sacred, which is
at the foundation of all religion. In every advancing civilization this sense of sacredness has found vigorous expression. It tends to retire into a recessive factor in experience,
as each phase of civilization enters upon its decay.

We are now discussing an alternative rendering of
Descartes' notion of perfection. It is the notion of that
power in history which implants into the form of process,
belonging to each historic epoch, the character of a drive
towards some ideal, to be realized within that period. This
ideal is never realized, it is beyond realization, and yet it
moulds the form of what is realized.

For example, there is an ideal of human liberty, activity, and coöperation dimly adumbrated in the American
Constitution. It has never been realized in its perfection;
and by its lack of characterization of the variety of possibilities open for humanity, it is limited and imperfect.
And yet, such as it is, the Constitution vaguely discloses
the immanence in this epoch of that one energy of idealiza-
tion, whereby bare process is transformed into glowing
history.

In this discussion we are upholding the thesis that the
sense of external reality—that is to say, the sense of being
one actuality in a world of actualities—is the gift of aes-

thetic significance. This experience claims a relevance beyond the finite immediacy of any one occasion of experience. If in that occasion, there is a failure consciously to discern that significance, so much the worse for that occasion. This doctrine applies to all experience, great and small. Our intuitions of righteousness disclose an absoluteness in the nature of things, and so does the taste of a *lump of sugar*.

The variations of importance are beyond our weak imaginations; and yet aesthetic importance in any factor of experience carries its proof of existence beyond present immediacy. The ego enjoys an importance stretching beyond itself.

The rise of animal, and then of human, consciousness is the triumph of specialization. It is closely connected with the evolution of clear and distinct sensory experience. There is abstraction from the vague mass of primary feelings, and concentration upon the comparative clarity of a few qualitative details. These are the sensa.

Unless the physical and physiological sciences are fables, the qualitative experiences which are the sensations, such as sight, hearing, etc., are involved in an intricate flux of reactions within and without the animal body. These are all hidden below consciousness in the vague sense of personal experience of an external world. This feeling is massive and vague—so vague that the pretentious phrase, namely, personal experience of an external world, sounds nonsense. A particular instance can be explained more simply. For example, "I see a blue stain out there," implies the privacy of the ego and the externality of "out there." There is the presupposition of "me" and the world beyond. But consciousness is concentrated on the quality blue in that position. Nothing can be more simple or more abstract. And yet unless the physicist and physiologist are talking nonsense, there is a terrific tale of complex activity omitted in the abstraction.

Further, our subsequent actions conform to the tales of the scientists, and not primarily to the blueness of the stain. We may want to preserve or modify the experience. But inexorably our actions are directive of our bodies. We do not touch the quality blue. We stretch out our arms to modify the relations of the blue thing to the various activities in its environment.

In so far as we are merely conscious of the formal relationships of qualities, there is aesthetic failure. It is the recognition of the arid fact of the possibility of relationship. The sense of reality is the sense of effectiveness, and the sense of effectiveness is the drive towards the satisfaction of appetition. There is a past, real in its own right, satisfying itself in the present.

10. Fact includes in its own nature something which is not fact, although it constitutes a realized item within fact. This is the conceptual side of fact. But, as usual, the philosophic tradition is too abstract. There is no such independent item in actuality as "mere concept." The concept is always clothed with emotion, that is to say, with hope, or with fear, or with hatred, or with eager aspiration, or with the pleasure of analysis. The variations in the quality of appetition are infinite. But the notion of mere concept, or of mere realization, apart from a relevant emotional derivation, which is its emotional origin, is fallacious. The doctrine here maintained is to be found in Hume, except that he oversimplifies the problem by conceiving an initial bare occurrence of sense-impressions devoid of essential relationship to other factors in experience. In his subsequent argument he is apt fortunately to forget his explicit premises. So it is possible to construe his meaning in many ways. But in his controversy with antagonistic modes of thought, he judges them by the strict consequences of these premises.

The final conclusion from the discussions included in this course of lectures is the importance of a right adjustment of the process of abstraction. Those characteristics of experience which separate the higher from the lower species of actualities all depend upon abstraction. The living germs are distinguished from lifeless physical activities by the abstractions inherent in their existence. The higher animals are distinguished from mere life, by their abstractions, and by their use of them. Mankind is distinguished from animal life by its emphasis on abstractions. The degeneracy of mankind is distinguished from its uprise by the dominance of chill abstractions, divorced from aesthetic content.

The growth of consciousness is the uprise of abstractions. It is the growth of emphasis. The totality is characterized by a selection from its details. That selection claims attention, enjoyment, action, and purpose, all relative to itself. This concentration evokes an energy of self-realization. It is a step towards unification with that drive towards realization which discloses the unity of aim in the historic process.

But this enhancement of energy presupposes that the abstraction is preserved with its adequate relevance to the concrete sense of value attainment from which it is derived. In this way, the effect of the abstraction stimulates the vividness and depth of the whole of experience. It stirs the depths.

Thus a fortunate use of abstractions is of the essence of upward evolution. But there is no necessity of such good use. Abstractions may function in experience so as to separate them from their relevance to the totality. In that case, the abstractive experience is a flicker of interest which is destroying its own massive basis for survival.

It is interesting to note that in the entertainment of

abstractions there is always present a preservative instinct aiming at the renewal of connection, which is the reverse of abstraction. This reverse process, partly instinctive and partly conscious, is wisdom of that higher life made possible by abstraction.

For example, in the consciousness of sense experience, we first fix attention on some sensory detail. We then glance around and attend to the environment of sights and sounds. We endeavour to lift into consciousness meaningful units, such as the whole picture, the whole building, the living animal, the stone, the mountain, the tree.

Such vivid conscious experience is a return to the concrete. The return may be misconceived. The abstraction may misdirect us as to the real complex from which it originates. But, in the dim recesses behind consciousness there is the sense of realities behind abstractions. The sense of process is always present. There is the process of abstraction arising from the concrete totality of value experience, and this process points back to its origin.

11. But consciousness, which is the supreme vividness of experience, does not rest content with the dumb sense of importance behind the veil. Its next procedure is to seek the essential connections within its own conscious area. This is the process of rationalization. This process is the recognition of essential connection within the apparent isolation of abstracted details. Thus rationalization is the reverse of abstraction, so far as abstraction can be reversed within the area of consciousness.

Our powers are finite. So, although no item in this process of reversion is necessarily beyond us, it is confined within the environment accidentally presented to us by our immediate area of consciousness. Thus rationalization is the partial fulfilment of the ideal to recover concrete reality within the disjunction of abstraction.

This disjunction is the appearance which has been

introduced as price of finite conscious discrimination. The concrete reality is the starting-point of the process of individual experience, and it is the goal in the rationalization of consciousness. The prize at the goal is the enhancement of experience by consciousness and rationality.

III.
NATURE AND LIFE

Nature Lifeless

*P*hilosophy is the product of wonder. The effort after the general characterization of the world around us is the romance of human thought. The correct statement seems so easy, so obvious, and yet it is always eluding us. We inherit the traditional doctrine: we can detect the oversights, the superstitions, the rash generalizations of the past ages. We know so well what we mean and yet we remain so curiously uncertain about the formulation of any detail of our knowledge. This word *detail* lies at the heart of the whole difficulty. You cannot talk vaguely about "Nature" in general. We must fix upon details within nature and discuss their essences and their types of inter-connection. The world around is complex, composed of details. We have to settle upon the primary types of detail in terms of which we endeavour to express our understanding of nature. We have to analyse and to abstract, and to understand the natural status of our abstractions. At first sight there are sharp-cut classes within which we can sort the various types of things and characters of things which we find in nature. Every age manages to find modes of classification which seem fundamental starting points for the researches of the special sciences. Each succeeding age discovers that the primary classifications of its predecessors will not work. In this way a doubt is thrown upon all formulations of laws of nature which assume these classifications as firm starting points. A problem arises. Philosophy is the search for the solution.

Our first step must be to define the term *nature* as here used. Nature, in these chapters, means the world as interpreted by reliance on clear and distinct sensory experiences, visual, auditory, and tactile. Obviously, such an interpretation is of the highest importance for human understanding. These final chapters are concerned with the question,—How far does it take us?

For example, we can conceive nature as composed of permanent things, namely bits of matter, moving about in space which otherwise is empty. This way of thinking about nature has an obvious consonance with common-sense observation. There are chairs, tables, bits of rock, oceans, animal bodies, vegetable bodies, planets, and suns. The enduring self-identity of a house, of a farm, of an animal body, is a presupposition of social intercourse. It is assumed in legal theory. It lies at the base of all literature. A bit of matter is thus conceived as a passive fact, an individual reality which is the same at an instant, or throughout a second, an hour, or a year. Such a material, individual reality supports its various qualifications such as shape, locomotion, colour, or smell, etc. The occurrences of nature consist in the changes in these qualifications, and more particularly in the changes of motion. The connection between such bits of matter consists purely of spatial relations. Thus the importance of motion arises from its change of the sole mode of interconnection of material things. Mankind then proceeds to discuss these spatial relations and discovers geometry. The geometrical character of space is conceived as the one way in which nature imposes determinate relations upon all bits of matter which are the sole occupants of space. In itself, space is conceived as unchanging from eternity to eternity, and as homogeneous from infinity to infinity. Thus we compose a straight-forward characterization of nature, which is consonant to common sense, and can be verified at each moment of our existence. We sit for hours in the same chair, in the same house, with the same animal body. The dimensions of the room are defined by its spatial relations. There are colours, sounds, scents, partly abiding and partly changing. Also the major facts of change are defined by locomotion of the animal bodies and of the inorganic furniture. Within this general concept of nature, there have somehow to be interwoven the further concepts of "Life" and "Mind."

I have been endeavouring to sketch the general common-sense notion of the universe, which about the beginning of the sixteenth century, say in the year 1500 A.D., was in process of formation among the more progressive thinkers of the European population. It was partly an inheritance from Greek thought and from medieval thought. Partly it was based on the deliverance of direct observation, at any moment verified in the world around us. It was the presupposed support supplying the terms in which the answers to all further questions were found. Among these further questions, the most fundamental and the most obvious are those concerning the laws of locomotion, the meaning of life, the meaning of mentality, and the interrelations of matter, life, and mentality. When we examine the procedures of the great men in the sixteenth and seventeenth centuries, we find them presupposing this general common-sense notion of the universe, and endeavouring to answer all questions in the terms it supplies.

I suggest that there can be no doubt, but that this general notion expresses large, all-pervading truths about the world around us. The only question is as to how fundamental these truths may be. In other words, we have to ask what large features of the universe cannot be expressed in these terms. We have also to ask whether we cannot find some other set of notions which will explain the importance of this common-sense notion, and will also explain its relations to those other features ignored by the common-sense notion.

When we survey the subsequent course of scientific thought throughout the seventeenth century up to the present day, two curious facts emerge. In the first place, the development of natural science has gradually discarded every single feature of the original common-sense notion. Nothing whatever remains of it, considered as expressing the primary features in terms of which the universe is to be interpreted. The obvious common-sense notion has been entirely destroyed, so far as concerns its function as the basis for all interpretation. One by one, every item has been dethroned.

There is a second characteristic of subsequent thought which is equally prominent. This common-sense notion still reigns supreme in the workaday life of mankind. It dominates the marketplace, the playgrounds, the law courts, and in fact the whole sociological intercourse of mankind. It is supreme in literature and is assumed in all the humanistic sciences. Thus the science of nature stands opposed to the presuppositions of humanism. Where some conciliation is attempted, it often assumes some sort of mysticism. But in general there is no conciliation.

Indeed, even when we confine attention to natural science, no special science ever is grounded upon the conciliation of presuppositions belonging to all the various

sciences of nature. Each science confines itself to a fragment of the evidence and weaves its theories in terms of
notions suggested by that fragment. Such a procedure is
necessary by reason of the limitations of human ability.
But its dangers should always be kept in mind. For example, the increasing departmentalization of universities
during the last hundred years, however necessary for ad-
ministrative purposes, tends to trivialize the mentality of
the teaching profession. The result of this effective survival
of two ways of thought is a patchwork procedure.

Presuppositions from the two points of view are interwoven sporadically. Every special science has to assume
results from other sciences. For example, biology presupposes physics. It will usually be the case that these loans
from one specialism to another really belong to the state
of science thirty or forty years earlier. The presuppositions
of the physics of my boyhood are today powerful influences
in the mentality of physiologists. Indeed we do not need
even to bring in the physiologists. The presuppositions of
yesterday's physics remain in the minds of physicists, although their explicit doctrines taken in detail deny them.

In order to understand this sporadic interweaving of
old and new in modern thought, I will recur to the main
principles of the old common-sense doctrine, which even
today is the common doctrine of ordinary life because in
some sense it is true. There are bits of matter, enduring
self-identically in space which is otherwise empty. Each bit
of matter occupies a definite limited region. Each such
particle of matter has its own private qualifications, such
as its shape, its motion, its mass, its colour, its scent. Some
of these qualifications change, others are persistent. The
essential relationship between bits of matter is purely
spatial. Space itself is eternally unchanging, always including in itself this capacity for the relationship of bits of

matter. Geometry is the science which investigates this spatial capacity for imposing relationship upon matter. Locomotion of matter involves change in spatial relationship. It involves nothing more than that. Matter involves nothing more than spatiality, and the passive support of qualifications. It can be qualified, and it must be qualified. But qualification is a bare fact, which is just itself. This is the grand doctrine of nature as a self-sufficient, meaningless complex of facts. It is the doctrine of the autonomy of physical science. It is the doctrine which in these lectures I am denying.

The state of modern thought is that every single item in this general doctrine is denied, but that the general conclusions from the doctrine as a whole are tenaciously retained. The result is a complete muddle in scientific thought, in philosophic cosmology, and in epistemology. But any doctrine which does not implicitly presuppose this point of view is assailed as unintelligible.

The first item to be abandoned was the set of qualifications which we distinguish in sense-perception, namely colour, sound, scent, and analogous qualifications. The transmission theories for light and sound, introduced the doctrine of secondary qualities. The colour and the sound were no longer in nature. They are the mental reactions of the percipient to internal bodily locomotions. Thus nature is left with bits of matter, qualified by mass, spatial relations, and the change of such relations.

This loss of the secondary qualities was a severe restriction to nature. For its value to the percipient was reduced to its function as a mere agent of excitement. Also the derived mental excitement was not primarily concerned with factors in nature. The colours and the sounds were secondary factors supplied by the mental reaction. But the curious fact remained that these secondary factors are perceived as related by the spatiality which is the grand substratum of nature. Hume was, I think, the first philosopher who explictly pointed out this curious hybrid character of our perceptions, according to the current doctrine of the perception of secondary qualities. Though of course this hybrid characteristic was tacitly presupposed by Locke when he conceived colour as a *secondary* quality of the things in nature. I believe that any cosmological doctrine which is faithful to the facts has to admit this artificial character of sense perception. Namely, when we perceive the red rose we are associating our enjoyment of red derived from one source with our enjoyment of a spatial region derived from another source. The conclusion that I draw is that sense perception for all its practical importance is very superficial in its disclosure of the nature of things. This conclusion is supported by the character of delusiveness—that is, of illusion—which persistently clings to sense perception. For example, our perception of stars which years ago may have vanished, our perceptions of images in mirrors or by refraction, our double vision, our visions under the influence of drugs. My quarrel with modern epistemology concerns its exclusive stress upon sense perception for the provision of data respecting nature. Sense perception does not provide the data in terms of which we interpret it.

This conclusion that pure sense perception does not provide the data for its own interpretation was the great discovery embodied in Hume's philosophy. This discovery is the reason why Hume's *Treatise* will remain as the irrefutable basis for all subsequent philosophic thought.

Another item in the common-sense doctrine concerns empty space and locomotion. In the first place, the transmission of light and sound shows that space apparently empty is the theatre of activities which we do not directly perceive. This conclusion was explained by the supposition of types of subtle matter, namely the ether, which we cannot directly perceive. In the second place, this conclusion, and the obvious behaviour of gross ordinary matter, show us that the motions of matter are in some way conditioned by the spatial relations of material bodies to each other. It was here that Newton supplied the great synthesis upon which science was based for more than two centuries. Newton's laws of motion provided a skeleton framework within which more particular laws for the interconnection of bodily motions could be inserted. He also supplied one example of such a particular law in his great law of gravitation, which depended upon mutual distances.

Newton's methodology for physics was an overwhelming success. But the forces which he introduced left nature still without meaning or value. In the essence of a material body—in its mass, motion, and shape—there was no reason for the law of gravitation. Even if the particular forces could be conceived as the accidents of a cosmic epoch, there was no reason in the Newtonian concepts of mass and motion why material bodies should be connected by any stress between them. Yet the notion of stresses, as essential connections between bodies, was a fundamental factor in the Newtonian concept of nature. What Newton left for empirical investigation was the determination of the particular stresses now existing. In this determination he made a magnificent beginning by isolating the stresses indicated by his law of gravitation. But he left no hint, why in the nature of things there should be any stresses at all. The arbitrary motions of the bodies were thus explained by the arbitrary stresses between material bodies, conjoined with their spatiality, their mass, and their initial states of motion. By introducing stresses—in particular the law of gravitation—instead of the welter of detailed transformations of motion, he greatly increased the systematic aspect of nature. But he left all the factors of the system—more particularly, mass and stress—in the position of detached facts devoid of any reason for their compresence. He thus illustrated a great philosophic truth, that a dead nature can give no reasons. All ultimate reasons are in terms of aim at value. A dead nature aims at nothing. It is the essence of life that it exists for its own sake, as the intrinsic reaping of value.

Thus for Newtonians, nature yielded no reasons: it could yield no reasons. Combining Newton and Hume we obtain a barren concept, namely a field of perception devoid of any data for its own interpretation, and a system of interpretation, devoid of any reason for the concurrence of its factors. It is this situation that modern philosophy from Kant onwards has in its various ways sought to render intelligible. My own belief is that this situation is a *reductio ad absurdum,* and should not be accepted as the basis for philosophic speculation. Kant was the first philosopher who in this way combined Newton and Hume. He accepted them both, and his three *Critiques* were his endeavour to render intelligible this Hume-Newton situation. But the Hume-Newton situation is the primary presupposition for all modern philosophic thought. Any endeavour to go behind it is, in philosophic discussion, almost angrily rejected as unintelligible.

My aim in these lectures is briefly to point out how both Newton's contribution and Hume's contribution are, each in their way, gravely defective. They are right as far as they go. But they omit those aspects of the universe as experienced, and of our modes of experiencing, which jointly lead to the more penetrating ways of understanding. In the recent situations at Washington, D.C., the Hume-Newton modes of thought can only discern a complex transition of sensa, and an entangled locomotion of molecules, while the deepest intuition of the whole world discerns the President of the United States inaugurating a new chapter in the history of mankind. In such ways the Hume-Newton interpretation omits our intuitive modes of understanding.

I now pass on to the influence of modern science in discrediting the remaining items of the primary common-sense notion with which science in the sixteenth century started its career. But in the present-day reconstruction of physics fragments of the Newtonian concepts are stubbornly retained. The result is to reduce modern physics to a sort of mystic chant over an unintelligible universe. This chant has the exact merits of the old magic ceremonies which flourished in ancient Mesopotamia and later in Europe. One of the earliest fragments of writing which has survived is a report from a Babylonian astrologer to the King, stating the favourable days to turn cattle into the fields, as deduced by his observations of the stars. This mystic relation of observation, theory, and practice, is exactly the present position of science in modern life, according to the prevalent scientific philosophy.

The notion of empty space, the mere vehicle of spatial interconnections, has been eliminated from recent science. The whole spatial universe is a field of force, or in other words, a field of incessant activity. The mathematical formulae of physics express the mathematical relations realized in this activity.

The unexpected result has been the elimination of bits of matter, as the self-identical supports for physical properties. At first, throughout the nineteenth century, the notion of matter was extended. The empty space was conceived as filled with ether. This ether was nothing else than the ordinary matter of the original common-sense notion. It had the properties of a jelly, with its continuity, its cohesion, its flexibility, and its inertia. The ordinary matter of common sense then merely represented certain exceptional entanglements in the ether—that is to say, knots in the ether. These entanglements, which are relatively infrequent throughout space, impose stresses and strains throughout the whole of the jelly-like ether. Also the agitations of ordinary matter are transmitted through the ether as agitations of the stresses and strains. In this way an immense unification was effected of the various doctrines of light, heat, electricity, and energy, which now coalesced into the one science of the ether. The theory was gradually elaborated throughout the nineteenth century by a brilliant group of physicists and mathematicians, French, German, Dutch, Scandinavian, British, Italian, American. The details of their work, and the relative contributions of various individuals are not to the point here.

The final result is that the activities of the ether are very different from any of the modes of activity which the common-sense analysis ascribes to ordinary matter. If the doctrine of ether be correct, then our ordinary notions of matter are derived from observations of certain average results which cloak the real nature of the activities of ether. The more recent revolution which has culminated in the physics of the present day has only carried one step further this trend of nineteenth century science. Its moral is the extreme superficiality of the broad generalizations which mankind acquires on the basis of sense perception. The continuous effort to understand the world has carried us far away from all those obvious ideas. Matter has been identified with energy, and energy is sheer activity; the passive substratum composed of self-identical enduring bits of matter has been abandoned, so far as concerns any fundamental description. Obviously this notion expresses an important derivative fact. But it has ceased to be the presupposed basis of theory. The modern point of view is expressed in terms of energy, activity, and the vibratory differentiations of space-time. Any local agitation shakes the whole universe. The distant effects are minute, but they are there. The concept of matter presupposed simple location. Each bit of matter was self-contained, localized in a region with a passive, static network of spatial relations, entwined in a uniform relational system from infinity to infinity and from eternity to eternity. But in the modern concept the group of agitations which we term matter is fused into its environment. There is no possibility of a detached, self-contained local existence. The environment enters into the nature of each thing. Some elements in the nature of a complete set of agitations may remain stable as those agitations are propelled through a changing environment. But such stability is only the case in a general, average way. This average fact is the reason why we find the same chair, the same rock, and the same planet, enduring for days, or for centuries, or for millions of years. In this average fact, then, time-factor takes the aspect of endurance, and change is a detail. The fundamental fact, according to the physics of the present day, is that the environment with its peculiarities seeps into the group-agitation which we term matter, and the group-agitations extend their character to the environment. In truth, the notion of the self-contained particle of matter, self-sufficient within its local habitation, is an abstraction. Now an abstraction is nothing else than the omission of part of the truth. The abstraction is well-founded when the conclusions drawn from it are not vitiated by the omitted truth.

This general deduction from the modern doctrine of physics vitiates many conclusions drawn from the applications of physics to other sciences, such as physiology, or even such as physics itself. For example, when geneticists conceive genes as the determinants of heredity. The analogy of the old concept of matter sometimes leads them to ignore the influence of the particular animal body in which they are functioning. They presuppose that a pellet of matter remains in all respects self-identical whatever be its changes of environment. So far as modern physics is concerned, any characteristics may, or may not, effect changes in the genes, changes which are as important in certain respects, though not in others. Thus no *a priori* argument as to the inheritance of characters can be drawn from the mere doctrine of genes. In fact recently physiologists have found that genes are modified in some respects by their environment. The presuppositions of the old common sense view survive, even when the view itself has been abandoned as a fundamental description.

This survival of fragments of older doctrines is also exemplified in the modern use of the term *space-time*. The notion of space with its geometry is strictly coördinated to the notion of material bodies with simple location in space. A bit of matter is then conceived as self-sufficient with the simple location of the region which it occupies. It is just there, in that region where it is; and it can be described without reference to the goings on in any other region of space. The empty space is the substratum for the passive geometrical relationships between material bodies. These relationships are bare, static facts and carry no consequences which are essentially necessary. For example, Newton's law of gravitation expresses the changes of locomotion which are associated with the spatial relations of material bodies with each other. But this law of gravitation does not result from the Newtonian notion of mass combined with the notion of the occupancy of space, together with the Euclidean geometry. None of these notions either singly or in combination give the slightest warrant for the law of gravitation. Neither Archimedes, nor Galileo, by puzzling over these notions could have derived any suggestion for the gravitational law. According to the doctrine, space was the substratum for the great all-pervading passive relationship of the natural world. It conditioned all the active relationships, but it did not necessitate them.

The new view is entirely different. The fundamental concepts are activity and process. Nature is divisible and thus extensive. But any division, including some activities and excluding others, also severs the patterns of process which extend beyond all boundaries. The mathematical formulae indicate a logical completeness about such patterns, a completeness which boundaries destroy. For example, half a wave tells only half the story. The notion of self-sufficient isolation is not exemplified in modern physics. There are no essentially self-contained activities within limited regions. These passive geometrical relationships between substrata passively occupying regions have passed out of the picture. Nature is a theatre for the interrelations of activities. All things change, the activities and their interrelations. To this new concept, the notion of space with its passive, systematic, geometric relationship is entirely inappropriate. The fashionable notion that the new physics has reduced all physical laws to the statement of geometrical relations is quite ridiculous. It has done the opposite. In the place of the Aristotelian notion of the procession of forms, it has substituted the notion of the forms of process. It has thus swept away space and matter, and has substituted the study of the internal relations within a complex state of activity. This complex state is in one sense a unity. There is the whole universe of physical action extending to the remotest star cluster. In another sense it is divisible into parts. We can trace interrelations within a selected group of activities, and ignore all other activities. By such an abstraction, we shall fail to explain those internal activities which are affected by changes in the external system which has been ignored. Also, in any fundamental sense, we shall fail to understand the retained activities. For these activities will depend upon a comparatively unchanging systematic environment.

In all discussions of nature we must remember the differences of scale, and in particular the differences of time-span. We are apt to take modes of observable functioning of the human body as setting an absolute scale. It is extremely rash to extend conclusions derived from observation far beyond the scale of magnitude to which observation was confined. For example, to exhibit apparent absence of change within a second of time tells nothing as to the change within a thousand years. Also no apparent change within a thousand years tells anything as to a million years; and no apparent change within a million years tells anything about a million million years. We can extend this progression indefinitely. There is no absolute standard of magnitude. Any term in this progression is large compared to its predecessor and is small compared to its successor.

Again, all special sciences presuppose certain fundamental types of things. Here I am using the word *thing* in its most general sense, which can include activities, colours and other sensa, and values. In this sense thing is whatever we can talk about. A science is concerned with a a limited set of various types of things. There is thus in the first place this variety of types. In the second place, there is the determination as to what types are exhibited in any indicated situation. For example, there is the singular proposition,—This is green; and the more general proposition,—All those things are green. This type of enquiry is what the traditional Aristotelian logic takes care of. Undoubtedly such enquiries are essential in the initial stage of any science. But every science strives to get beyond it. Unfortunately, owing to the way in which for over two thousand years philosophic thought has been dominated by its background of Aristotelian logic, all attempts to combine the set of special sciences into a philosophic cosmology, giving some understanding of the universe—all these attempts are vitiated by an unconscious relapse into these Aristotelian forms as the sole mode of expression. The disease of philosophy is its itch to express itself in the forms, "Some S is P," or "All S is P."

Returning to the special sciences, the third step is the endeavour to obtain quantitative decisions. In this stage, the typical questions are, "How much P is involved in S" and "How many S's are P?" In other words, number, quantity, and measurement, have been introduced. A simple-minded handling of these quantitative notions can be just as misleading as undue trust in the Aristotelian forms for propositions.

The fourth stage in the development of the science is the introduction of the notion of pattern. Apart from attention to this concept of pattern, our understanding of nature is crude in the extreme. For example, given an aggregate of carbon atoms and oxygen atoms, and given that the number of oxygen atoms and the number of carbon atoms are known, the properties of the mixture are unknown until the question of pattern is settled. How much free oxygen is there,—How much free carbon,—How much carbon monoxide,—How much carbon dioxide? The answers to some of these questions, with the total quantities of oxygen and of carbon presupposed, will determine the answer to the rest. But even allowing for this mutual determination,

there will be an enormous number of alternative patterns
for a mixture of any reasonable amount of carbon and
oxygen. And even when the purely chemical pattern is
settled, and when the region containing the mixture is
given, there are an indefinite number of regional patterns
for the distribution of the chemical substances within the
containing region. Thus beyond all questions of quantity,
there lie questions of pattern, which are essential for the
understanding of nature. Apart from a presupposed pattern, quantity determines nothing. Indeed quantity itself
is nothing other than analogy of functions within analogous patterns.

Also this example, involving mere chemical mixture,
and chemical combination, and the seclusion of different
substances in different subregions of the container, shows
us that notion of pattern involves the concept of different
modes of togetherness. This is obviously a fundamental
concept which we ought to have thought of as soon as we
started with the notion of various types of fundamental
things. The danger of all these fundamental notions is that
we are apt to assume them unconsciously. When we ask
ourselves any question we will usually find that we are
assuming certain types of entities involved, that we are
assuming certain modes of togetherness of these entities,
and that we are even assuming certain widely spread generalities of pattern. Our attention is concerned with details
of pattern, and measurement, and proportionate magnitude. Thus the laws of nature are merely all-pervading
patterns of behaviour, of which the shift and discontin-
uance lie beyond our ken. Again, the topic of every science
is an abstraction from the full concrete happenings of
natures. But every abstraction neglects the influx of the
factors omitted into the factors retained. Thus a single
pattern discerned by vision limited to the abstractions

within a special science differentiates itself into a subordinate factor in an indefinite number of wider patterns when we consider its possibilities of relatedness to the omitted universe. Even within the circle of the special science we may find diversities of functioning not to be explained in terms of that science. But these diversities can be explained when we consider the variety of wider relationships of the pattern in question.

Today the attitude among many leaders in natural science is a vehement denial of the considerations which have been put forward. Their attitude seems to me to be a touching example of baseless faith. This judgment is strengthened when we reflect that their position of the autonomy of the natural sciences has its origin in a concept of the world of nature, now discarded.

Finally, we are left with a fundamental question as yet undiscussed. What are those primary types of things in terms of which the process of the universe is to be understood? Suppose we agree that nature discloses to the scientific scrutiny merely activities and process. What does this mean? These activities fade into each other. They arise and then pass away. What is being enacted? What is effected? It cannot be that these are merely the formulae of the multiplication table—in the words of a great philosopher, merely a bloodless dance of categories. Nature is fullblooded. Real facts are happening. Physical nature, as studied in science, is to be looked upon as a complex of the more stable interrelations betwen the real facts of the real universe.

This lecture has been confined to nature under an abstraction in which all reference to life was suppressed. The effect of this abstraction has been that dynamics, physics, and chemistry were the sciences which guided our gradual transition from the full common-sense notions of the sixteenth century to the concept of nature suggested by the speculative physics of the present day.

This change of view, occupying four centuries, may be characterized as the transition from space and matter, as the fundamental notions to process conceived, as a complex of activity with internal relations between its various factors. The older point of view enables us to abstract from change and to conceive of the full reality of nature *at an instant,* in abstraction from any temporal duration and characterized as to its interrelations solely by the instantaneous distribution of matter in space. According to the Newtonian view, what had thus been omitted was the change of distribution at neighbouring instants. But such change was, on this view, plainly irrelevant to the essential reality of the material universe at the instant considered. Locomotion, and change of relative distribution, was accidental and not essential.

Equally accidental was endurance. Nature at an instant is, in this view, equally real whether or not there be no nature at any other instant, or indeed whether or not there be any other instant. Descartes, who with Galileo and Newton, cooperated in the construction of the final Newtonian view, accepted this conclusion. For he explained endurance as perpetual re-creation at each instant. Thus the matter of fact was, for him, to be seen in the instant and not in the endurance. For him, endurance was a mere succession of instantaneous facts. There were other sides to Descartes' cosmology which might have led him to a greater emphasis on motion. For example, his doctrines of extension and vortices. But in fact, by anticipation, he drew the conclusion which fitted the Newtonian concepts.

There is a fatal contradiction inherent in the Newtonian cosmology. Only one mode of the occupancy of space is allowed for—namely, this bit of matter occupying this region at this durationless instant. This occupation of space is the final real fact, without reference to any other instant, or to any other piece of matter, or to any other region of space. Now assuming this Newtonian doctrine, we ask—What becomes of velocity, at an instant? Again we ask—What becomes of momentum at an instant? These notions are essential for Newtonian physics, and yet they are without any meaning for it. Velocity and momentum require the concept that the state of things at other times and other places enter into the essential character of the material occupancy of space at any selected instant. But the Newtonian concept allows for not such modification of the relation of occupancy. Thus the cosmological scheme is inherently inconsistent. The mathematical subtleties of the differential calculus afford no help for the removal of this difficulty. We can indeed phrase the point at issue in mathematical terms. The Newtonian notion of occupancy corresponds to the value of a function at a selected point. But the Newtonian physics requires solely the limit of the function at that point. And the Newtonian cosmology gives no hint why the bare fact which is the value should be replaced by the reference to other times and places which is the limit.

For the modern view process, activity, and change are the matter of fact. At an instant there is nothing. Each instant is only a way of grouping matters of fact. Thus since there are no instants, conceived as simple primary entities, there is no nature at an instant. Thus all the interrelations of matters of fact must involve transition in their essence. All realization involves implication in the creative advance.

The discussion in this lecture is only the prolegomenon for the attempt to answer the fundamental question,—

How do we add content to the notion of bare activity? Activity for what, producing what, activity involving what?

The next lecture will introduce the concept of life, and will thus enable us to conceive of nature more concretely, without abstraction.

Nature Alive

The status of life in nature, as defined in the previous chapter, is the modern problem of philosophy and of science. Indeed it is the central meeting point of all the strains of systematic thought, humanistic, naturalistic, philosophic. The very meaning of life is in doubt. When we understand it, we shall also understand its status in the world. But its essence and its status are alike baffling.

After all, this conclusion is not very different from our conclusion respecting nature, considered in abstraction from the notion of life. We were left with the notion of an activity in which nothing is effected. Also this activity, thus considered, discloses no ground for its own coherence. There is merely a formula for succession. But there is an absence of understandable causation to give a reason for that formula for that succession. Of course it is always possible to work oneself into a state of complete contentment with an ultimate irrationality. The popular positivistic philosophy adopts this attitude.

The weakness of this positivism is the way in which we all welcome the detached fragments of explanation attained in our present stage of civilization. Suppose that a hundred thousand years ago our ancestors had been wise positivists. They sought for no reasons. What they had observed was sheer matter of fact. It was the development of no necessity. They would have searched for no reasons underlying facts immediately observed. Civilization would never have developed. Our varied powers of detailed observation of the world would have remained dormant. For the peculiarity of a reason is that the intellectual development of its consequences suggests consequences beyond the topics already observed. The extension of observation waits upon some dim apprehension of reasonable connection. For example, the observation of insects on flowers dimly suggests some congruity between the natures of insects and of flowers, and thus leads to a wealth of observation from which whole branches of science have developed. But a consistent positivist should be content with the observed facts, namely insects visiting flowers. It is a fact of charming simplicity. There is nothing further to be said upon the matter, according to the doctrine of a positivist. At present the scientific world is suffering from a bad attack of muddle-headed positivism, which arbitrarily applies its doctrine and arbitrarily escapes from it. The whole doctrine of life in nature has suffered from this positivist taint. We are told that there is the routine described in physical and chemical formulae, and that in the process of nature there is nothing else.

The origin of this persuasion is the dualism which gradually developed in European thought in respect to mind and nature. At the beginning of the modern period Descartes expresses this dualism with the utmost distinctness. For him, there are material substances with spatial relations, and mental substances. The mental substances are external to the material substances. Neither type requires the other type for the completion of its essence. Their unexplained interrelations are unnecessary for their respective existences. In truth, this formulation of the problem in terms of minds and matter is unfortunate. It omits the lower forms of life, such as vegetation and the lower animal types. These forms touch upon human mentality at their highest, and upon inorganic nature at their lowest.

The effect of this sharp division between nature and life has poisoned all subsequent philosophy. Even when the coördinate existence of the two types of actualities is abandoned, there is no proper fusion of the two in most modern schools of thought. For some, nature is mere appearance and mind is the sole reality. For others, physical nature is the sole reality and mind is an epiphenomenon. Here the phrases "mere appearance" and "epiphenomenon" obviously carry the implication of slight importance for the understanding of the final nature of things.

The doctrine that I am maintaining is that neither physical nature nor life can be understood unless we fuse them together as essential factors in the composition of "really real" things whose interconnections and individual characters constitute the universe.

The first step in the argument must be to form some concept of what life can mean. Also we require that the deficiencies in our concept of physical nature should be supplied by its fusion with life. And we require that, on the other hand, the notion of life should involve the notion of physical nature.

Now as a first approximation the notion of life implies a certain absoluteness of self-enjoyment. This must mean a certain immediate individuality, which is a complex process of appropriating into a unity of existence the many data presented as relevant by the physical processes of nature. Life implies the absolute, individual self-enjoyment arising out of this process of appropriation. I have, in my recent writings, used the word *prehension* to express this process of appropriation. Also I have termed each individual act of immediate self-enjoyment an *occasion of experience*. I hold that these unities of existence, these occasions of experience, are the really real things which in their collective unity compose the evolving universe, ever plunging into the creative advance.

But these are forward references to the issue of the argument. As a first approximation we have conceived life as implying absolute, individual self-enjoyment of a process of appropriation. The data appropriated are provided by the antecedent functioning of the universe. Thus the occasion of experience is absolute in respect to its immediate self-enjoyment. How it deals with its data is to be understood without reference to any other concurrent occasions. Thus the occasion, in reference to its internal process, requires no contemporary process in order to exist. In fact this mutual independence in the internal process of self-adjustment is the definition of contemporaneousness.

This concept of self-enjoyment does not exhaust that aspect of process here termed *life*. Process for its intelligibility involves the notion of a creative activity belonging to the very essence of each occasion. It is the process of eliciting into actual being factors in the universe which antecedently to that process exist only in the mode of unrealized potentialities. The process of self-creation is the transformation of the potential into the actual, and the fact of such transformation includes the immediacy of self-enjoyment.

Thus in conceiving the function of life in an occasion of experience, we must discriminate the actualized data presented by the antecedent world, the non-actualized potentialities which lie ready to promote their fusion into a new unity of experience, and the immediacy of self-enjoyment which belongs to the creative fusion of those data with those potentialities. This is the doctrine of the creative advance whereby it belongs to the essence of the universe, that it passes into a future. It is nonsense to conceive of nature as a static fact, even for an instant devoid of duration. There is no nature apart from transition, and there is no transition apart from temporal duration. This is the reason why the notion of an instant of time, conceived as a primary simple fact, is nonsense.

But even yet we have not exhausted the notion of creation which is essential to the understanding of nature. We must add yet another character to our description of life. This missing characteristic is "aim." By this term *aim* is meant the exclusion of the boundless wealth of alternative potentiality, and the inclusion of that definite factor of novelty which constitutes the selected way of entertaining those data in that process of unification. The aim is at that complex of feeling which is the enjoyment of those data in that way. "That way of enjoyment" is selected from the boundless wealth of alternatives. It has been aimed at for actualization in that process.

Thus the characteristics of life are absolute self-enjoyment, creative activity, aim. Here aim evidently involves the entertainment of the purely ideal so as to be directive of the creative process. Also the enjoyment belongs to the process and is not a characteristic of any static result. The aim is at the enjoyment belonging to the process.

The question at once arises as to whether this factor of life in nature, as thus interpreted, corresponds to anything that we observe in nature. All philosophy is an endeavour to obtain a self-consistent understanding of things observed. Thus its development is guided in two ways, one is the demand for a coherent self-consistency, and the other is the elucidation of things observed. It is therefore our first task to compare the above doctrine of life in nature with our direct observations.

Without doubt the sort of observations most prominent

in our conscious experience are the sense perceptions. Sight, hearing, taste, smell, touch, constitute a rough list of our major modes of perception through the senses. But there are an indefinite set of obscure bodily feelings which form a background of feeling with items occasionally flashing into prominence. The peculiarity of sense perception is its dual character, partly irrelevant to the body and partly referent to the body. In the case of sight, the irrelevance to the body is at its maximum. We look at the scenery, at a picture, or at an approaching car on the road, as an external presentation given for our mental entertainment or mental anxiety. There it is, exposed to view. But on reflection, we elicit the underlying experience that we were seeing with our eyes. Usually this fact is not in explicit consciousness at the moment of perception. The bodily reference is recessive, the visible presentation is dominant. In the other modes of sensation, the body is more prominent. There is great variation in this respect between the different modes. In any doctrine as to the information derived from sense perception this dual reference, external reference and bodily reference, should be kept in mind. The current philosophic doctrines, mostly derived from Hume, are defective by reason of their neglect of bodily reference. Their vice is the deduction of a sharp-cut doctrine from an assumed sharp-cut mode of perception. The truth is that our sense perceptions are extraordinarily vague and confused modes of experience. Also there is every evidence that their prominent side of external reference is very superficial in its disclosure of the universe. It is important. For example, pragmatically a paving stone is a hard, solid, static, irremoveable fact. This is what sense perception, on its sharp-cut side, discloses. But if physical science be correct, this is a very superficial account of that portion of the universe which we call the paving stone. Modern physical science is the issue of a coördinated effort, sustained for more than three centuries, to understand those activities of nature by reason of which the transitions of sense perception occur.

Two conclusions are now abundantly clear. One is that sense perception omits any discrimination of the fundamental activities within nature. For example, consider the difference between the paving stone as perceived visually, or by falling upon it, and the molecular activities of the paving stone as described by the physicist. The second conclusion is the failure of science to endow its formulae for activity with any meaning. The divergence of the formulae about nature from the appearance of nature has robbed the formulae of any explanatory character. It has even robbed us of reason for believing that the past gives any ground for expectation of the future. In fact, science conceived as resting on mere sense perception, with no other source of observation, is bankrupt, so far as concerns its claim to self-sufficiency.

Science can find no individual enjoyment in nature: Science can find no aim in nature: Science can find no creativity in nature; it finds mere rules of succession. These negations are true of natural science. They are inherent in its methodology. The reason for this blindness of physical science lies in the fact that such science only deals with half the evidence provided by human experience. It divides the seamless coat—or, to change the metaphor into a happier form, it examines the coat, which is superficial, and neglects the body which is fundamental.

The disastrous separation of body and mind which has been fixed on European thought by Descartes is responsible for this blindness of science. In one sense the abstraction has been a happy one, in that it has allowed the simplest things to be considered first, for about ten generations. Now these simplest things are those widespread habits of nature that dominate the whole stretch of the universe within our remotest, vaguest observation. None of these laws of nature gives the slightest evidence of necessity. They are the modes of procedure which within the scale of our observations do in fact prevail. I mean, the fact that the extensiveness of the universe is dimensional, the fact that the number of spatial dimensions is three, the spatial laws of geometry, the ultimate formulae for physical occurrences. There is no necessity in any of these ways of behaviour. They exist as average, regulative conditions because the majority of actualities are swaying each other to modes of interconnection exemplifying those laws. New modes of self-expression may be gaining ground. We cannot tell. But, to judge by all analogy, after a sufficient span of existence our present laws will fade into unimportance. New interests will dominate. In our present sense of the term, our spatio-physical epoch will pass into the background of the past, which conditions all things dimly and without evident effect on the decision of prominent relations.

These massive laws, at present prevailing, are the general physical laws of inorganic nature. At a certain scale of observation they are prevalent without hint of interference. The formation of suns, the motions of planets, the geologic changes on the earth, seem to proceed with a massive impetus which excludes any hint of modification by other agencies. To this extent sense perception on which science relies discloses no aim in nature.

Yet it is untrue to state that the general observation of mankind, in which sense perception is only one factor, discloses no aim. The exact contrary is the case. All explanations of the sociological functionings of mankind include aim as an essential factor in explanation. For example, in a criminal trial where the evidence is circumstantial the demonstration of motive is one chief reliance of the prosecution. In such a trial would the defence plead the doctrine that purpose could not direct the motions of the body, and that to indict the thief for stealing was analogous to indicting the sun for rising? Again no statesman can conduct international relations without some estimate—implicit or explicit in his consciousness—of the types of patriotism respectively prevalent in various nations and in the statesmen of these nations. A lost dog can be seen trying to find his master or trying to find his way home. In fact we are *directly* conscious of our purposes as *directive* of our actions. Apart from such direction no doctrine could in any sense be acted upon. The notions entertained mentally would have no effect upon bodily actions. Thus what happens would happen in complete indifference to the entertainment of such notions.

Scientific reasoning is completely dominated by the presupposition that mental functionings are not properly part of nature. Accordingly it disregards all those mental antecedents which mankind habitually presuppose as effective in guiding cosmological functionings. As a method this procedure is entirely justifiable, provided that we recognize the limitations involved. These limitations are both obvious and undefined. The gradual eliciting of their definition is the hope of philosophy.

The points that I would emphasize are, first, that this sharp division between mentality and nature has no ground in our fundamental observation. We find ourselves living within nature. Secondly, I conclude that we should conceive mental operations as among the factors which make up the constitution of nature. Thirdly, that we should reject the notion of idle wheels in the process of nature. Every factor which emerges makes a difference, and that difference can only be expressed in terms of the individual character of that factor. Fourthly, that we have now the task of defining natural facts, so as to understand how mental occurrences are operative in conditioning the subsequent course of nature.

A rough division can be made of six types of occurrences in nature. The first type is human existence, body and mind. The second type includes all sorts of animal life, insects, the vertebrates, and other genera. In fact all the various types of animal life other than human. The third type includes all vegetable life. The fourth type consists of the single living cells. The fifth type consists of all large scale inorganic aggregates, on a scale comparable to the size of animal bodies, or larger. The sixth type is composed of the happenings on an infinitesimal scale, disclosed by the minute analysis of modern physics.

Now all these functionings of nature influence each other, require each other, and lead on to each other. The list has purposely been made roughly, without any scientific pretension. The sharp-cut scientific classifications are essential for scientific method. But they are dangerous for philosophy. Such classification hides the truth that the different modes of natural existence shade off into each other. There is the animal life with its central direction of a society of cells, there is the vegetable life with its organized republic of cells, there is the cell life with its organized republic of molecules, there is the large-scale inorganic society of molecules with its passive acceptance of necessities derived from spatial relations, there is the inframolecular activity which has lost all trace of the passivity of inorganic nature on a larger scale.

In this survey some main conclusions stand out. One conclusion is the diverse modes of functioning which are produced by diverse modes of organization. The second conclusion is the aspect of continuity between these different modes. There are borderline cases, which bridge the gaps. Often the borderline cases are unstable, and pass quickly. But span of existence is merely relative to our habits of human life. For inframolecular occurrence, a second is a vast period of time. A third conclusion is the difference in the aspects of nature according as we change the scale of observation. Each scale of observation presents us with average effects proper to that scale.

Again, another consideration arises. How do we observe nature? Also, what is the proper analysis of an observation? The conventional answer to this question is that we perceive nature through our senses. Also in the analysis of sense perception we are apt to concentrate upon its most clear-cut instance, namely sight. Now visual perception is the final product of evolution. It belongs to high-grade animals—to vertebrates and to the more advanced type of insects. There are numberless living things which afford no evidence of possessing sight. Yet they show every sign of taking account of their environment in the way proper to living things. Also human beings shut off sight with peculiar ease, by closing our eyes or by the calamity of blindness. The information provided by mere sight is peculiarly barren—namely external regions disclosed as coloured. There is no necessary transition of colours, and no necessary selection of regions, and no necessary mutual adaptation of the display of colours. Sight at any instant merely provides the passive fact of regions variously coloured. If we have memories, we observe the transition of colours. But there is nothing intrinsic to the mere coloured regions which provides any hint of internal activity whereby change can be understood. It is from this experience that our conception of a spatial distribution of passive material substances arises. Nature is thus described as made up of vacuous bits of matter with no internal values, and merely hurrying through space.

But there are two accompaniments of this experience which should make us suspicious of accepting it at its face value as any direct disclosure of the metaphysical nature of things. In the first place, even in visual experience we are also aware of the intervention of the body. We know directly that we see *with our eyes*. That is a vague feeling, but extremely important. Secondly, every type of crucial experiment proves that what we see, and where we see it, depend entirely upon the physiological functioning of our body. Any method of making our body function internally in a given way, will provide us with an assigned visual sensation. The body is supremely indifferent to the happenings of nature a short way off, where it places its visual sensa.

Now the same is true of all other modes of sensation, only to a greater extent. All sense perception is merely one outcome of the dependence of our experience upon bodily functionings. Thus if we wish to understand the relation of our personal experience to the activities of nature, the proper procedure is to examine the dependence of our personal experiences upon our personal bodies.

Let us ask about our overwhelming persuasions as to our own personal body-mind relation. In the first place, there is the claim to unity. The human individual is one fact, body and mind. This claim to unity is the fundamental fact, always presupposed, rarely explicitly formulated. I am experiencing and my body is mine. In the second place, the functioning of our body has a much wider influence than the mere production of sense experience. We find ourselves in a healthy enjoyment of life by reason of the healthy functionings of our internal organs—heart, lungs, bowels, kidneys, etc. The emotional state arises just because they are not providing any sensa directly associated with themselves. Even in sight, we enjoy our vision because there is no eyestrain. Also we enjoy our general state of life, because we have no stomachache. I am insisting that the enjoyment of health, good or bad, is a positive feeling only casually associated with particular sensa. For example, you can enjoy the ease with which your eyes are functioning even when you are looking at a bad picture or a vulgar building. This direct feeling of the derivation of emotion from the body is among our fundamental experiences. There are emotions of various types— but every type of emotion is at least modified by derivation from the body. It is for physiologists to analyse in detail the modes of bodily functioning. For philosophy, the one fundamental fact is that the whole complexity of mental experience is either derived or modified by such functioning. Also our basic feeling is this sense of derivation, which leads to our claim for unity, body and mind.

But our immediate experience also claims derivation from another source, and equally claims a unity founded upon this alternative source of derivation. This second source is our own state of mind directly preceding the immediate present of our conscious experience. A quarter of a second ago, we were entertaining such and such ideas, we were enjoying such and such emotions, and we were making such and such observations of external fact. In our present state of mind, we are continuing that previous state. The word *continuing* states only half the truth. In one sense it is too weak, and in another sense it overstates. It is too weak, because we not only continue, but we claim absolute identity with our previous state. It was our very identical self in that state of mind, which is of course the basis of our present experience a quarter of a second later. In another sense the word *continuing* overstates. For we do not quite continue in our preceding state of experience. New elements have intervened. All of these new elements are provided by our bodily functionings. We fuse these new elements with the basic stuff of experience provided by our state of mind a quarter of a second ago. Also, as we have already agreed, we claim an identification with our body. Thus our experience in the present discloses its own nature as with two sources of derivation, namely, the body and the antecedent experiential functionings. Also there is a claim for identification with each of these sources. The body is mine, and the antecedent experience is mine. Still more, there is only one ego, to claim the body and to claim the stream of experience. I submit that we have here the fundamental basic persuasion on which we found the whole practice of our existence. While we exist, body and soul are inescapable elements in our being, each with the full reality of our own immediate self. But neither body nor soul possesses the sharp observational definition which at first sight we attribute to them. Our knowledge of the body places it as a complex unity of happenings within the larger field of nature. But its demarcation from the rest of nature is vague in the extreme. The body consists of the coördinated functionings of billions of molecules. It belongs to the structural essence of the body that, in an indefinite number of ways, it is always losing molecules and gaining molecules. When we consider the question with microscopic accuracy, there is no definite boundary to determine where the body begins and external nature ends. Again the body can lose whole limbs, and yet we claim identity with the same body. Also the vital functions of the cells in the amputated limb ebb slowly. Indeed the limb survives in separation from the body for an immense time compared to the internal vibratory periods of its molecules. Also apart from such catastrophes, the body requires the environment in order to exist. Thus there is a unity of the body with the environment, as well as a unity of body and soul into one person.

But in conceiving our personal identity we are apt to emphasize rather the soul than the body. The one individual is that coördinated stream of personal experiences, which is my thread of life or your thread of life. It is that succession of self-realization, each occasion with its direct memory of its past and with its anticipation of the future. That claim to enduring self-identity is our self-assertion of personal identity.

Yet when we examine this notion of the soul, it discloses itself as even vaguer than our definition of the body. First, the continuity of the soul—so far as concerns consciousness—has to leap gaps in time. We sleep or we are stunned. And yet it is the same person who recovers consciousness. We trust to memory, and we ground our trust on the continuity of the functionings of nature, more especially on the continuity of our body. Thus nature in general and the body in particular provide the stuff for the personal endurance of the soul. Again there is a curious variation in the vividness of the successive occasions of the soul's existence. We are living at full stretch with a keen observation of external occurrence; then external attention dies away and we are lost in meditation; the meditation gradually weakens in vivid presentation: we doze; we dream; we sleep with a total lapse of the stream of consciousness. These functionings of the soul are diverse, variable, and discontinuous. The claim to the unity of the soul is analogous to the claim to the unity of the body, and is analogous to the claim to the unity of body and soul, and is analogous to the claim to the community of the body with an external nature. It is the task of philosophic speculation to conceive the happenings of the universe so as to render understandable the outlook of physical science and to combine this outlook with these direct persuasions representing the basic facts upon which epistemology must build. The weakness of the epistemology of the eighteenth and nineteenth centuries was that it based itself purely upon a narrow formulation of sense perception. Also among the various modes of sensation, visual experience was picked out as the typical example. The result was to exclude all the really fundamental factors constituting our experience.

In such an epistemology we are far from the complex data which philosophic speculation has to account for in a system rendering the whole understandable. Consider the types of community of body and soul, of body and nature, of soul and nature, or successive occasions of bodily existence, or the soul's existence. These fundamental interconnections have one very remarkable characteristic. Let us ask what is the function of the external world for the stream of experience which constitute the soul. This world, thus experienced, is the basic fact within those experiences. All the emotions, and purposes, and enjoyments, proper to the individual existence of the soul are nothing other than the soul's reactions to this experienced world which lies at the base of the soul's existence.

Thus in a sense, the experienced world is one complex factor in the composition of many factors constituting the essence of the soul. We can phrase this shortly by saying that in one sense the world is in the soul.

But there is an antithetical doctrine balancing this primary truth. Namely, our experience of the world involves the exhibition of the soul itself as one of the components within the world. Thus there is a dual aspect to the relationship of an occasion of experience as one relatum and the experienced world as another relatum. The world is included within the occasion in one sense, and the occasion is included in the world in another sense. For example, I am in the room, and the room is an item in my present experience. But my present experience is what I now am.

But this baffling antithetical relation extends to all the connections which we have been discussing. For example, consider the enduring self-identity of the soul. The soul is nothing else than the succession of my occasions of experience, extending from birth to the present moment. Now, at this instant, I am the complete person embodying all these occasions. They are mine. On the other hand it is equally true that my immediate occasion of experience, at the present moment, is only one among the stream of occasions which constitutes my soul. Again, the world for me is nothing else than how the functionings of my body present it for my experience. The world is thus wholly to be discerned within those functionings. Knowledge of the world is nothing else than an analysis of the functionings. And yet, on the other hand, the body is merely one society of functionings within the universal society of the world. We have to construe the world in terms of the bodily society, and the bodily society in terms of the general functionings of the world.

Thus, as disclosed in the fundamental essence of our experience, the togetherness of things involves some doctrine of mutual immanence. In some sense or other, this community of the actualities of the world means that each happening is a factor in the nature of every other happening. After all, this is the only way in which we can understand notions habitually employed in daily life. Consider our notion of causation. How can one event be the cause of another? In the first place, no event can be wholly and solely the cause of another event. The whole antecedent world conspires to produce a new occasion. But some one occasion in an important way conditions the formation of a successor. How can we understand this process of conditioning?

The mere notion of transferring a quality is entirely unintelligible. Suppose that two occurrences may be in fact detached so that one of them is comprehensible without reference to the other. Then all notion of causation between them, or of conditioning, becomes unintelligible. There is—with this supposition—no reason why the possession of any quality by one of them should in any way influence the possession of that quality, or of any other quality, by the other. With such a doctrine the play and interplay of qualitative succession in the world becomes a blank fact from which no conclusions can be drawn as to past, present, or future, beyond the range of direct observation. Such a positivistic belief is quite self-consistent, provided that we do not include in it any hopes for the future or regrets for the past. Science is then without any importance. Also effort is foolish, because it determines nothing. The only intelligible doctrine of causation is founded on the doctrine of immanence. Each occasion presupposes the antecedent world as active in its own nature. This is the reason why events have a determinate status relatively to each other. Also it is the reason why the qualitative energies of the past are combined into a pattern of qualitative energies in each present occasion. This is the doctrine of causation. It is the reason why it belongs to the essence of each occasion that it is *where* it is. It is the reason for the transference of character from occasion to occasion. It is the reason for the relative stability of laws of nature, some laws for a wider environment, some laws for a narrower environment. It is the reason why—as we have already noted—in our direct apprehension of the world around us we find that curious habit of claiming a twofold unity with the observed data. We are in the world and the world is in us. Our immediate occasion is in the society of occasions forming the soul, and our soul is in our present occasion. The body is ours, and we are an activity within our body. This fact of observation, vague but imperative, is the foundation of the connexity of the world, and of the transmission of its types of order.

In this survey of the observational data in terms of which our philosophic cosmology must be founded, we have brought together the conclusions of physical science, and those habitual persuasions dominating the sociological functionings of mankind. These persuasions also guide the humanism of literature, of art, and of religion. Mere existence has never entered into the consciousness of man, except as the remote terminus of an abstraction in thought. Descartes' "Cogito, ergo sum" is wrongly translated, "I *think,* therefore I am." It is never bare thought or bare existence that we are aware of. I find myself as essentially a unity of emotions, enjoyments, hopes, fears, regrets, valuations of alternatives, decisions—all of them subjective reactions to the environment as active in my nature. My unity—which is Descartes' "I am"—is my process of shaping this welter of material into a consistent pattern of feelings. The individual enjoyment is what I am in my role of a natural activity, as I shape the activities of the environment into a new creation, which is myself at this moment; and yet, as being myself, it is a continuation of the antecedent world. If we stress the role of the environment, this process is causation. If we stress the role of my immediate pattern of active enjoyment, this process is self-creation. If we stress the role of the conceptual anticipation of the future whose existence is a necessity in the nature of the present, this process is the teleological aim at some ideal in the future. This aim, however, is not really beyond the present process. For the aim at the future is an enjoyment in the present. It thus effectively conditions the immediate self-creation of the new creature.

We can now again ask the final question as put forward at the close of the former lecture. Physical science has reduced nature to activity, and has discovered abstract mathematical formulae which are illustrated in these activities of nature. But the fundamental question remains, How do we add content to the notion of bare activity? This question can only be answered by fusing life with nature.

In the first place, we must distinguish life from mentality. Mentality involves conceptual experience, and is only one variable ingredient in life. The sort of functioning here termed *conceptual experience* is the entertainment of possibilities for ideal realization in abstraction from any sheer physical realization. The most obvious example of conceptual experience is the entertainment of alternatives. Life lies below this grade of mentality. Life is the enjoyment of emotion, derived from the past and aimed at the future. It is the enjoyment of emotion which was then, which is now, and which will be then. This vector character is of the essence of such entertainment.

The emotion transcends the present in two ways. It issues from, and it issues towards. It is received, it is enjoyed, and it is passed along, from moment to moment. Each occasion is an activity of concern, in the Quaker sense of that term. It is the conjunction of transcendence and immanence. The occasion is concerned, in the way of feeling and aim, with things that in their own essence lie beyond it; although these things in their present functions are factors in the concern of that occasion. Thus each occasion, although engaged in its own immediate self-realization, is concerned with the universe.

The process is always a process of modification by reason of the numberless avenues of supply, and by reason of the numberless modes of qualitative texture. The unity of emotion, which is the unity of the present occasion, is a patterned texture of qualities, always shifting as it is passed into the future. The creative activity aims at preservation of the components and at preservation of intensity. The modifications of pattern, the dismissal into elimination, are in obedience to this aim.

In so far as conceptual mentality does not intervene, the grand patterns pervading the environment are passed on with the inherited modes of adjustment. Here we find the patterns of activity studied by the physicists and chemists. Mentality is merely latent in all these occasions as thus studied. In the case of inorganic nature any sporadic flashes are inoperative so far as our powers of discernment are concerned. The lowest stages of effective mentality, controlled by the inheritance of physical pattern, involves the faint direction of emphasis by unconscious ideal aim. The various examples of the higher forms of life exhibit the variety of grades of effectiveness of mentality. In the social habits of animals, there is evidence of flashes of mentality in the past which have degenerated into physical habits. Finally in the higher mammals and more particularly in mankind, we have clear evidence of mentality habitually effective. In our own experience, our knowledge consciously entertained and systematized can only mean such mentality, directly observed.

The qualities entertained as objects in conceptual activity are of the nature of catalytic agents, in the sense in which that phrase is used in chemistry. They modify the aesthetic process by which the occasion constitutes itself out of the many streams of feeling received from the past. It is not necessary to assume that conceptions introduce additional sources of measurable energy. They may do so; for the doctrine of the conservation of energy is not based upon exhaustive measurements. But the operation of mentality is primarily to be conceived as a diversion of the flow of energy.

In these lectures I have not entered upon systematic metaphysical cosmology. The object of the lectures is to indicate those elements in our experience in terms of which such a cosmology should be constructed. The key notion from which such construction should start is that the energetic activity considered in physics is the emotional intensity entertained in life.

Philosophy begins in wonder. And, at the end, when philosophic thought has done its best, the wonder remains. There have been added, however, some grasp of the im-

mensity of things, some purification of emotion by understanding. Yet there is a danger in such reflections. An immediate good is apt to be thought of in the degenerate form
of a passive enjoyment. Existence is activity ever merging
into the future. The aim at philosophic understanding is
the aim at piercing the blindness of activity in respect to
its transcendent functions.

The Aim of Philosophy

The task of a university is the creation of the future, so far as rational thought, and civilized modes of appreciation, can affect the issue. The future is big with every possibility of achievement and of tragedy.

Amid this scene of creative action, What is the special function of philosophy?

In order to answer this question, we must first decide what constitutes the philosophic character of any particular doctrine. What makes a doctrine philosophical? No one truth, thoroughly understood in all the infinitude of its bearings, is more or less philosophical than any other truth. The pursuit of philosophy is the one avocation denied to omniscience.

Philosophy is an attitude of mind towards doctrines ignorantly entertained. By the phrase "ignorantly entertained" I mean that the full meaning of the doctrine in respect to the infinitude of circumstances to which it is relevant, is not understood. The philosophic attitude is a resolute attempt to enlarge the understanding of the scope of application of every notion which enters into our current thought. The philosophic attempt takes every word, and

every phrase, in the verbal expression of thought, and asks,
What does it mean? It refuses to be satisfied by the conventional presupposition that every sensible person knows the
answer. As soon as you rest satisfied with primitive ideas,
and with primitive propositions, you have ceased to be a
philosopher.

Of course you have got to start somewhere for the purposes of discourse. But the philosopher, as he argues from
his premises, has already marked down every word and
phrase in them as topics for future enquiry. No philosopher
is satisfied with the concurrence of sensible people, whether
they be his colleagues, or even his own previous self. He
is always assaulting the boundaries of finitude.

The scientist is also enlarging knowledge. He starts
with a group of primitive notions and of primitive relations between these notions, which defines the scope of his
science. For example, Newtonian dynamics assumes Euclidean space, massive matter, motion, stresses and strains,
and the more general notion of force. There are also the
laws of motion, and a few other concepts added later. The
science consisted in the deduction of consequences, presupposing the applicability of these ideas.

In respect to Newtonian dynamics, the scientist and the
philosopher face in opposite directions. The scientist asks
for the consequences, and seeks to observe the realization
of such consequences in the universe. The philosopher asks
for the meaning of these ideas in terms of the welter of
characterizations which infest the world.

It is evident that scientists and philosophers can help
each other. For the scientist sometimes wants a new idea,
and the philosopher is enlightened as to meanings by the
study of the scientific consequences. Their usual mode of
intercommunication is by sharing in the current habits of
cultivated thought.

There is an insistent presupposition continually sterilizing philosophic thought. It is the belief, the very natural belief, that mankind has consciously entertained all the fundamental ideas which are applicable to its experience. Further it is held that human language, in single words or in phrases, explicitly expresses these ideas. I will term this presupposition, "The Fallacy of the Perfect Dictionary."

It is here that the philosopher, as such, parts company with the scholar. The scholar investigates human thought and human achievement, armed with a dictionary. He is the main support of civilized thought. Apart from scholarship, you may be moral, religious, and delightful. But you are not wholly civilized. You will lack power of delicate accuracy of expression.

It is obvious that the philosopher needs scholarship, just as he needs science. But both science and scholarship are subsidiary weapons for philosophy.

The fallacy of the perfect dictionary divides philosophers into two schools, namely, the "Critical School," which repudiates speculative philosophy, and the "Speculative School" which includes it. The critical school confines itself to verbal analysis within the limits of the dictionary. The speculative school appeals to direct insight, and endeavours to indicate its meanings by further appeal to situations which promote such specific insights. It then enlarges the dictionary. The divergence between the schools is the quarrel between safety and adventure.

The strength of the critical school lies in the fact that the doctrine of evolution never entered, in any radical sense, into ancient scholarship. Thus there arises the presupposition of a fixed specification of the human mind; and the blue print of this specification is the dictionary.

I appeal to two great moments in the history of philosophy. Socrates spent his life in analysing the current presuppositions of the Athenian world. He explicitly recognized that his philosophy was an attitude in the face of ignorance. He was critical and yet constructive.

Harvard is justly proud of the great period of its philosophic department about thirty years ago. Josiah Royce, William James, Santayana, George Herbert Palmer, Münsterberg, constitute a group to be proud of. Among them Palmer's achievements centre chiefly in literature and in his brilliance as a lecturer. The group is a group of men individually great. But as a group they are greater still. It is a group of adventure, of speculation, of search for new ideas. To be a philosopher is to make some humble approach to the main characterstic of this group of men.

The use of philosophy is to maintain an active novelty of fundamental ideas illuminating the social system. It reverses the slow descent of accepted thought towards the inactive commonplace. If you like to phrase it so, philosophy is mystical. For mysticism is direct insight into depths as yet unspoken. But the purpose of philosophy is to rationalize mysticism: not by explaining it away, but by the introduction of novel verbal characterizations, rationally coördinated.

Philosophy is akin to poetry, and both of them seek to express that ultimate good sense which we term civilization. In each case there is reference to form beyond the direct meanings of words. Poetry allies itself to metre, philosophy to mathematic pattern.

Index

Index

Printed in the United States
By Bookmasters